T0149524

DIARY OF A BATTERED WOMAN

What Was She Thinking? Why Did She Stay?

Richard Lopez

DIARY OF A BATTERED WOMAN
WHAT WAS SHE THINKING? WHY DID SHE STAY?

iUniverse books may be ordered through booksellers or by contacting:

iUniverse
1663 Liberty Drive
Bloomington, IN 47403
www.iuniverse.com
1-800-Authors (1-800-288-4677)

ISBN: 978-1-5320-3707-8 (sc)
ISBN: 978-1-5320-3706-1 (e)

Library of Congress Control Number: 2017917461

Print information available on the last page.

iUniverse rev. date: 01/10/2018

for jenna

DID YOU SEE HOW SHE
LOOKED THIS MORNING"

"SHE SAID THAT SHE FELL,
BUT I DON'T I THINK SO"

"WHY DOES SHE STAY
WITH HIM, WHAT WAS
SHE THINKING"

man kills wife,
his children,
and himself.

Dallas, Mar.2 1994
Susan Johnson, 31
And her two children
Were shot to death
By her husband, Scott
Johnson, 34 yesterday
Afternoon. When the
Police arrived they
Found Scott dead
From a self inflicted
Wound.

Much has been written about domestic violence and the effect it has on its victims. There are many statistics being published, such as how victims of domestic violence constitute the number one cause of women being treated at hospital emergency wards. Also there are many facts concerning the number of incidents, the percentages relative to other numerical facts, and so forth. I am not going to bore you with numbers in this book. What you will find are the experiences and thoughts of a real person. A person, who, through her entries in her diary, will share with you her thoughts and feelings as she experienced them.

Rita grew up in a house with her mother Margaret, her father, who can remain nameless, sister Barbara and younger brother Mike. As far back as she can remember, her father battered her mother. As far back as she could remember Rita's father was very strict with her. He always criticized the way she dressed and always blamed her mother. There were even times when Rita spilled food on herself or the table, he would slap her mother as if a girl of five years old could always be neat. He also was always getting angry when Rita cried for whatever reason. Rita didn't realize at the time that there were other fathers that didn't behave any different than her's. Mostly it was her mother Margaret who was the victim of her father's abuse. Whenever her father battered her mother Rita would want to stop the violence by crying but it never really succeeded. Sometimes Rita became very sad because she thought that she was to blame for her mother being yelled at or hit. Sometimes the fights started after her father reprimanded her for something she did wrong. Rita remembered as if it were yesterday when one night she wet the bed and her father went into a rage and yelled profanities at Margaret because he said that she was not teaching Rita how to get up in the middle of the night to go to the bathroom. Rita was only six years old. Sometimes it seemed like they were going to have a nice day, like the day they were all going for a ride. Happy days didn't usually last long because the arguments always started and since Rita had to sit between her mother and father, she sometimes was hit on her face by accident with a glancing blow by her father's arm. It did not seem to Rita as that she was the intended target. And as if the violence she witnessed was not enough, seeing her mother become a shadow of who she was, pained her the most. The trauma of hiding in closets and under beds to keep out of harms way was the most terrifying. Rita dreamed of someday being able to marry a nice man who would love her and have a home and family of her own. Her chance came when her father had been arrested, served two years on drug convictions, and after being released, went away with another woman and had not been seen or heard from since. Rita's mother lived with her 17 year old son, Rita's brother, and his girlfriend. Rita's father would probably have interfered with Rita meeting someone. If nothing else he would interfere just to harass and bother Margaret. While not perfect, Rita looked forward to marrying a man like Jim, a 26 year old man she met when he delivered furniture to someone in the apartment building where she lived. Rita saw Jim as the "strong and silent" type, believing that this characteristic was what she admired in a man. She didn't even know at, at this point, what his name was.

MAY, 18 1995

Today, finally I can write something interesting. I think he likes me, His name is Jim and he asked me if I had a telephone, and when I told him that I didn't he said he would pass by after work.

MAY 19 1995

Jim passed by today. I made sure he saw me. Jim parked his delivery truck and got out. There is something about his strength and his assertiveness that I like. I think that I like a man who can love me and take care of me.

COMMENTARY

Maybe in a subconscious manner, Rita was attracted to a man that would enable her to not have to decide things. There is a possibility that her father, as cruel as he may have been, caused Rita to believe that a family needed a man who would make decisions. Jim would love her and be good to her, so she thought.

No doubt, the other more popular factors would come into play, such as rugged good looks, strong, and the ability to say the right things as far as Rita was concerned. Jim did not possess a high degree of intelligence or maybe it was a lack of ambition or even a kind of disinterest in academics. Jim simply did not have the discipline to study or plan for any kind of career. Jim did have what would be a good personality for some woman, in this case, Rita.

Sept. 9 1995

Its all been so great. Jim and I have been dating since we met, and I think I should get married with him. Today, the final summer weekend we went to the beach and Jim said that he liked me.

Sept. 11 1995

Today Jim stayed home from work, because he was angry with his boss and decided to make a long weekend of it. Tonight we'll go to the movies. It's not always good to have someone make all the decisions because we always had to see what Jim wanted to see. I didn't seem to be able to question it.

I guess that's a small price to pay for being so happy.

COMMENTARY

All men do not appeal to all women and vice a versa. Rita's passiveness attracted Jim, and Jim's characteristics, while not appealing to most women, did to Rita. So as long as Jim felt that he was in control, he was happy. The control over things that he felt was his to control gave him a sense of power. As long as Rita submitted to this hunger for power and control, things could go reasonably well. The problem is that it seemed as if Rita had to continue feeding him an ever increasing amount of herself, of her own needs and desires.

The relationship was unbalanced, tilted, away from equality. A functional relationship thrives within a circle of equality (domestic violence project, Duluth, Minnesota)). Within this circle, parties are loving, share decisions and possibly more important, the desire to please a partner in his needs. When both do this, the outcome is a balance that keeps both sort of orbiting around each other without a center that is tilted toward one or the other. In Jim and Rita's world, the imbalance placed Jim in the center, creating a feeling of insignificance in Rita.

Oct. 2 1995

Jim wants me to live with him and I really want to. Maybe I can get him to marry me. Tomorrow I'm going to talk to my mother about it. If I can get a job maybe, I can help my family. I know that I can help Jim with buying things for our house.

Oct. 3 1995

My mom and I were so happy today. We talked a lot about living with Jim. We both think that maybe we could get married. My mom just wants me to be happy and to have a better life than the one she says she had.

Nov. 13 1995

Jim wants me to stay with him today. I guess people don't wear wedding gowns or have parties anymore. I will stay with him and make him a nice home.

COMMENTARY

The pattern sets in early in their relationship. The giving up of childhood dreams that begin when young girls play house. Little girls who grow up in an environment where there is no violence at home play house and imitate grown ups and the games are happy often using play kitchens and doll houses. Rita did not have opportunities to play at being a housewife, believing, or knowing, that in the future the most she could aspire to, was to have someone make this dream of family and home a reality. Jim appeared to be that person. When Rita suggested that maybe they could finally get married, Jim became angry. In an attempt to appear to agree with Jim she said that it was her mother's idea anyway. Jim looked furious, stared at Rita and with his finger pointed very close to her nose, told her to tell her mother to stay out of his business. One of the characteristics of wanting or having power is to alienate the partner from a support base. In Rita's case the support would come from her family and Jim was not going to allow any power sharing with her family.

Dec. 1 1995

When Jim was convinced that getting married was his idea, he suggested that they do so,

Today Jim and I went on a honeymoon. We went to a hotel on the beach. After washing up we went to the lounge in the hotel. They had a singer who played the piano. Jim asked me to dance but I really thought he had too many drinks because when we did dance, he kept losing his balance. I laughed when he stepped on my toes. Instead of laughing he became irritated at my little bit of laughter and his mood changed quickly. He started to criticize everything about me. Later as he continued to reproach me for what he said was my disrespect I became afraid to look at him. When I scanned the room, he said I was looking at another man. Jim grabbed my arm and practically pulled me along the hallway and once in the bathroom, he slapped me on my face. I was terrified and kept quite when he told me if he ever caught me with or looking at another man he would kill me. I pretended to be sleepy and told him that I was going to take a shower. Jim left the room saying that he would be right back. As I showered I noticed the redness on my arm and still could feel the sting of the slap on my face. I pretended to be sleeping when he returned. He could hardly stand and fell on the bed, falling asleep immediately.

DEC. 2 1995

I woke up hearing the shower. I felt a pain in my chest, not from anything physical, but from anxiousness, fear and depression. These feelings disappeared when Jim, smiling, said that he wanted to take me to breakfast. Throughout breakfast Jim was as pleasant as ever. When the waitress brought the menu to us Jim told me to order whatever i desired. My sense of well being at that moment actually made me hungry. I ordered two scrambled eggs, two slices of bacon, and pancakes. Jim ordered the same. He said he was sorry about last night and said that he loved me a lot and wants me to just love him. Today after breakfast we went to the park. We had great fun and later we returned to his house, which I guess it's mine too now. Everything seems perfect now.

Commentary

Jim, like many abusive men, conduct a pattern of behavior that appears to follow a cycle. This cycle, the cycle of violence (domestic violence project, Duluth, Minnesota) usually consist of three phases, the tension building phase, the physical violence phase and the honeymoon phase.

Rita experienced this cycle for the first time when Jim began to criticize her every actions and continued when he began to accuse her of looking another man. This all culminated in his slapping her in the hotel bath room The next morning when Jim treated her well, he was going through the honeymoon phase. What triggered this behavior? There are those that believe that the perception that he is losing the power that he wants to feel, and the control that it brings, causes him to lash out at his mate. This loss could be as a result of a feeling of inadequacy or a sub- conscious feeling of inferiority. The next day feeling better about himself, he apologized and treated Rita better.

The cycle repeats itself over and over, each time going through its phases faster. Not that Rita did not experience moments of happiness, even though sometimes not being in fear, even momentarily, was confused with happiness. The days became weeks and the weeks became months. What appeared to Rita to be an unbearable disappointment, seemed to be an endless time of ups and downs.

During the Thanksgiving and Christmas holidays there were many unhappy moments, even without major physical incidents, because Jim did not allow Rita to shop freely with her mother as she had done in the past. Whenever they could they went to the better stores and spent hours looking at clothes and then ending up at a discount store to buy what they could. During the month of January 1996, Jim could not find the television remote. He called out to Rita where's the clicker. Rita replied that he was the last to use it. Jim became frustrated because he couldn't find it and began to holler at Rita. A Hey bitch find me the fucking clicker. Rita told Jim that he probably let it fall between the cushions on the sofa. Jim then grabbed Rita by her hair and pulled her to the sofa. When I tell you to do something you better do it. Rita reached in between the cushions where Jim usually sat and after feeling for it, she grabbed it and gave it to Jim saying A here's your clicker. Jim suddenly slapped Rita across the face and much to his surprise, and to her's, she slapped him back. Jim's eyes became glazed and Rita became terrified. As he approached her, she panicked and ran to the bedroom. Jim followed her to the bedroom and was in such a rage that he had trouble opening the door that Rita had no time to lock. Now crazed with anger, Jim entered the room and grabbed Rita by her hair and punched her about three times on her face with his fist. As Jim battered Rita he threatened her saying I'll teach you who's the boss around here and I'll kill you bitch.While being struck on her face, Rita kept asking Jim not to hit her again and that she was sorry and wouldn't do it again. By now Rita didn't even know what she was apologizing for. Jim went into the living room and turned on the television set. Rita went, sobbing, into the bathroom to tend to her wounds. Several minutes later Jim went to the bathroom and wiped her face with a warm cloth and told her that he was sorry about the black eye she had, but that she just had to learn to listen. He hugged her and they both went to bed. Jim to sleep and Rita to stay awake to think about her pain and what to do about the bruises on her face. The next morning Jim got up as if nothing happened and went to work. Rita spent the morning picking up things and cleaned the house. When she began to prepare dinner she made sure that she used groceries that she already had, to avoid going to the supermarket where most of the workers there knew her and would notice what had happened to her. Rita also called her mother but her mother sensed that something was wrong. Rita cut the conversation short and told her mother that she would call her tomorrow. Rita did not want her mother to know about something that her mother knew so well.

JAN. 11 1996

Yesterday Jim hurt me but later he tried to help me clean my face. Maybe I should have just looked for the t.v. remote. I don't know what got into me when I slapped Jim. I couldn't beat him in a fight if I tried.

Commentary

Two things occurred as a result of this last incident. One was the realization on the part of Rita that if she physically fought back she would invariably get hurt even more. Jim would have to assert his control over Rita by demonstrating a more violent behavior in order to instill more fear in her. The other point was that even though he appeared to apologize to Rita, he did so in a way that left the feeling that she was at fault anyway by not listening to him. And as if to reward her for understanding him, he went into a honeymoon phase by tending to her bruises. Feb. 2 1996

I can't wait to tell my mother that i'm pregnant, but I better tell Jim first. I think he is going to be so happy to hear that he is going to be a father. At least I hope he will. Something tells me that with a baby in our family Jim is going to treat me and the baby really well, and that maybe this will be the start of something new and good

COMMENTARY

Jim did take the news that he was going to be a father well. He excitedly wanted to buy everything that a baby needed all at once, even though he was far from having enough money to do it with. Nevertheless, Rita enjoyed a period of relative peace. There were even moments that seemed impossible to imagine just a few weeks ago. Jim had told Rita that he didn't mind if her mother took care of the baby when they went out, and even said that he wondered what Rita's brother Mike would buy for the baby.

MAY. 27 1996

Jim went bowling with friends from work. He said that after I have the baby, I can go with him. Right now I'm not in shape to bowl. What really bothered me was when he said that I looked too out of shape to hang around with him in public. He's being influenced by his friends. I wish that I could know who is going with him. I'm writing this at two in the morning and if Jim ever found this diary, he would kill me. I can't help wanting to write in the diary, It's kind of like talking to myself in a sane kind of way. I wonder what time he's going to come home.

COMMENTARY

When Jim got home at about 4:00 a.m., It was hard for Rita to believe that he was bowling for so many hours. Jim had obviously been drinking, and when Rita asked him where he had been, he became angry. Rita kept quite and Jim fell asleep right away mumbling something about A talk to you about where I've been in the morning.

COMMENTARY

Fear can be a friend or an enemy. It's a friend when fear gets you out of harms way, such as described in the fight or flight syndrome. But it's an enemy when it paralyzes a person and prevents someone from doing what is in the persons best interest. In Rita's case, after that one incident where she thought to strike back, and after it turned out to cause a terrible beating, she lacked the will to even think of fighting Jim again.

In Rita's case she was failing to develop an identity. Fear caused her to not consider her choices about anything. If Jim used his uncanny ability to manipulate Rita as an advertising executives manipulates the buying public, he would be a top notch sales pro. The problem was that Jim wasn't aware of his abusive behavior or even if he intended or planned any of his abusive behavior. Except when he purposely intimidated her to bring her into line, as he described his actions to himself. Actually he formed his violent characteristics many years ago. Jim must have either cared for someone very much who always talked tough or seemed to be fearless or seemed to be in control of everything around him. A manner of behavior that shaped Jim's life. Of course Jim could hardly control anyone. He wasn't smart enough to control anyone by success in the business world, and he wasn't strong enough to frighten his friends or even his enemies. But Rita was perfect, she was like other woman he had met, who gave him the respect that he so much wanted. Of course this came at a price. The price was having to instill your will on your mate on a daily basis lest you find yourself losing control and having to regain lost ground in the war to impose your will on someone else, and in Jim's case Rita.

The next morning, Jim came into the kitchen where Rita was and asked, no, demanded coffee. Rita knew immediately that Jim was not satisfied that she did not complain or mention anything about where he was the night before. Fear began to take over Rita's emotions and a sensation of heat rising to her head as the rest of her trembled. No sooner did Rita place the cup of coffee on the table when Jim used the color of the coffee as an excuse to release his pent-up anger. An anger that he could define as being directed at Rita but in reality, there was nothing she could have done right to prevent the violence that had just begun. Jim, struck the coffee cup with the back of his hand, sending it flying against the stove, shattering and spilling coffee all over the floor. As Rita bent to pick up the pieces of broken glass, Jim got up and kicked her in the buttocks, causing Rita to strike her head against the stove. It almost seemed as if Jim was annoyed that Rita had started to clean up the mess before he Actually told her to do so, he began to scream at Rita demanding that she clean the floor anyway. Rita told Jim "I *am* cleaning the floor," not as a confrontation, but in the false belief that maybe Jim did not realize that she was already doing it. This infuriated Jim. A Don't you answer me back A Jim grabbed Rita's hair and slapped her twice on her face. In what seemed to Rita to be a life saving decision, for her. Jim put on his shoes and left. Later, Rita got dressed and went to her mother's house for lack of knowing where else to go. Rita did though, have many misgivings about involving her family. When Rita got to her mother's house, she began to cry uncontrollably. Fortunately, Rita had no visible marks, the redness had subsided. The mother and daughter had discussed whether or not to call the police, stay with her or even to go to the hospital to find out if what happened had an effect on her pregnancy. Several hours later Jim showed up and knocked on the door. Rita's mother afraid, told Jim to go away or she would call the police. Jim began to yell profanities and to bang on the door. Rita told her mother that if she didn't open the door, someone would call the police, and things could get worse. When she opened the door, Jim entered scowled at Rita's mother, grabbed Rita by her arm and stated to anyone who may or may not have been listening, "my woman belongs to me." Did he really mean *with* me or *to* me? Once home, Jim became somewhat nice to Rita, given that he satisfied for the moment his power and control urge, and that now he would enter a honeymoon phase. Rita fell asleep long after Jim. Rita has many thoughts about her shattered dreams and whether or not Jim loved her.

JUNE 5, 1996

I don't know if Jim loves me. Will He change after the baby is born? If he doesn't love me now, will he then, I hope so.

COMMENTARY

It appears at the very least that Jim did not love Rita. The very question as to what love is, can be disputed. Jim and Rita, as most people, have an image of who and what they want in a person. This image can be just below the awareness threshold. In Rita's case, the part of her image that she did not allow to surface was the expectation that the man that she married would for one thing, get her out of the house and take care of her. The part that she did allow to surface was that he would build a home with her and have a family. That surface image matched Jim's surface image; a vision he had of himself as the respected man of the house. So they appeared to be in love, when in reality it seemed to be a marriage of convenience in that Rita's subconscious desire to have a strong man take care of her, as her father did with her mother, was being satisfied. Jim also had suppressed hidden desires. Jim did not think about how he felt inadequate, and more shamefully, (to him) a realization that he had certain sexual dysfunctions, the nature of which need not be mentioned because of the extreme variations of what can go wrong. Especially since Jim, who already had this desire to imitate somebody who had a strong influence on him, could not admit his shortcomings to himself. Rather then love Rita Jim used her to fulfill his desires, to make him feel as the knight in shining armor. It was as if Jim was in a movie in his mind, and he was the hero. The problem is that in this movie Rita is given a script to read. Rita's script called for her to be humiliated, humbled, hurt physically and emotionally. All of this to enhance the role played in Jim's mind's movie. Naturally, when things did not go as Jim wanted in the real world, that=s when things became dangerous for Rita.

Even if at times it seemed to Rita that she could not endure a life of broken dreams and maybe worst, broken skin and severe bruises, the months went by, as so did the summer and fall of 1996. There were incidents where Rita experienced being pushed and slapped but for the most part nothing major occurred. Understanding of course that what is minor to one person is major to someone else. Depending on their up bringing and or their disposition, some people cry if just yelled at and others do not even consider being lightly struck by someone as battery.

This pattern continued until September 6 1996. On this date, there were some teenage boys throwing a football along side Jim=s 1991 ford pick up truck. The football was overthrown and the boy who made a tremendous effort to catch it, let it bounce off his hands and harmlessly onto the back of the pick up. Jim began to yell at the boys and when the boys taunted him, he picked up a small piece of wood that he had in his truck, and threw it at the boys who were running away. The stick hit one of the boys on his head. It was a glancing blow that the boy rubbed and then continued to run. When Rita saw the piece of wood strike the boy, she screamed out of fear for the boy but also out of fear that the boy would comeback with his father or someone else that could cause this incident to escalate. The matter could have ended there. The boy did not appear to be hurt and did not return. No harm was done to Jim's truck. But it did not end there. Even if he didn't admit it to himself, Jim felt as though Rita had sided with this kid, who not only could have damaged his truck but who had the audacity to laugh at him from a safe distance. When Jim and Rita returned to their apartment, Jim immediately began to call Rita names and to accuse her of going to bed with all the young boys in the neighborhood. "I'll show you to disrespect me." Jim suddenly struck Rita on her face with his fist. It wasn't a slap this time, but a closed fist punch that caught Rita on her face just in front of her ear. In a panic she tried to get away but Jim hit her on the back of her head with his fist. My god, she thought he's hitting me as if I were a man. "stop your going to hurt me." "Hurt you," I'm going to beat the living shit out of you, you whore" Jim continued to hit Rita with his fist on her arms. Rita fell, or was she just trying to show Jim that he was hitting her more then normal, and he might take pity on her now that she was on the floor. That was not to be the case. Jim began to yell at Rita to get up as he commenced kicking her wherever his foot found her. Rita could not believe that Jim did not care that she was pregnant. Rita realized that Jim didn't care if he killed the unborn baby. The baby was the furthest thing from his mind at the moment. In a panic, Rita picked up the telephone and dialed 911. Jim grabbed the telephone and pulled the wires out of the wall receptacle. Rita then ran into the bathroom. She managed to lock the door just as Jim reached the door. Jim ordered Rita to open the door. Rita knew by now that if she didn't, Jim would perceive that he was not in control and that would really set him into a rage. Rita was torn between opening the door and hoping that Jim would calm down and not opening the door to prevent being harmed further. She especially did not want to jeopardize the baby. She tried to stay calm for the babies sake believing that if she could control her panic, the baby would not suffer. After a while, Jim began to bang on the bathroom door harder and harder. It was only a matter of time for the door to break. Jim hollered that if she didn't open the door he would break it down. The door frame was moving back and forth with each blow from Jim's fist. Rita thought that in a moment the part of the door frame that holds the lock and door knob was about to give. Suddenly she heard someone knocking on the door. It's the police open the door. Using technology that allows the police dispatcher to know the address of whoever is calling, the dispatcher sent a police unit to the address. When the police heard the banging on the door and Jim demanding that Rita open the door, they knew that a domestic violence incident was in progress. When the police believe that someone is being harmed and that a crime is in progress, they can enter a dwelling without a warrant and without being invited. Usually whoever is on the inside will open the door preferring to take their chances with talking there way out of trouble. When Jim opened the door the first of the two officers, the male one asked Jim if they could come in, allowing them time to assess the overall scene. Upon entering the police immediately split up with the male officer asking Jim what was happening. Jim replied to the officers question saying that nothing was wrong, that they had just been arguing and that he would never lay a finger on his wife.. The female officer went to the bathroom door and told Rita that is was okay to open the door, that it was safe. The female officer saw the redness on Rita's face. Very often when the police arrive at the scene of a domestic violence incident, the black and blue marks have not developed yet. That comes later. Nevertheless, the police officer knew that Rita had been battered. The female police officer asked Rita the same question and Rita agreed, that they were only having a loud argument. The police officer told them both that a call had been made and that was why they responded. Rita, embarrassed stated that she did not know anything about a telephone call.

Rita thought it better to get caught in a lie then the wrath of Jim's anger. The police asked many other questions among them if he had hit Rita while she was obviously pregnant. Jim replied that he had not, that he knew that she was pregnant and that he would never hit his pregnant wife. The police at this point who had already decided to arrest Jim, would raise the charge from a simple battery to a felony (aggravated) battery. In most states the police do not require that the victim in a domestic violence case press charges. No longer can the police or society for that matter, deem that the violence is a family matter. Many states require that its police officers make an arrest if they have reasonable suspicion that the violence took place and that the person they suspect actually did it. The police arrest report also mentioned that the defendant had redness on his knuckles. As the male officer placed Jim under arrest and began to handcuff him, the female police officer went to talk to Rita, who was now crying uncontrollably. She kept screaming at the police to not take Jim and that she had hurt herself. (A point that Jim would use in court in the future.) The female police officer knew what Rita had gone through, she had responded to hundreds of similar situations. The police officer told Rita that she needed to do something to protect herself and her future baby. The police officer than gave Rita a leaflet, as most police departments are required to do, indicating where the petitioner can go to obtain help. The female police officer took photographs of Rita's bruises as possible future evidence. The police drove off with Jim in the back seat, but not before Rita made one last attempt to get Jim freed and maybe to let Jim know that she was on his side. Rita cried for a while and when the tears stopped her fear continued. Rita did not know what would happen to Jim. Rita called her mother for advice. All she got from her mother was an explanation of what was going to happen and that she should understand that men are sometimes "like that" The next morning Rita called some of the numbers that were on the flyer, not for help for herself, but to see what she could do to help Jim. Whenever she spoke to someone on then telephone she would not admit to him that Jim was in jail. She would refer to what happened as having a "problem" last night and that her husband had gone with the police. Not mentioning that Jim had actually been arrested. Right after one of her calls, the telephone rang and it was Jim. Much to her surprise, Jim was actually nice to her saying that he world never do it again. He also asked her to call the State Attorney's office to tell them that it was all a mistake.In some States the State Attorney's Office is called the District Attorney. Also he asked her to go a bond hearing at noon to tell the judge that she knows that it won't happen again. The hearing is held before a judge so that the judge can determine if there was probable cause for the arrest and if so, to determine under what conditions he could be released and the amount of bail is set for the defendants release. At about two o'clock in the afternoon they called Jim's name. Jim appeared, disheveled from a night in a holding cell. Rita was terrified at speaking to a judge but was more terrified not to. There are various ways that the state can handle a situation where the victim pleads for mercy for the abuser. In this case the judge scolded Jim and told him that he will still have to answer to the charges, but that he will allow him to post bail and allow him to return to his home, and that he better not hear that he laid a finger on Rita. Rita felt that she had done all she could for Jim but more importantly Jim would know that she did. Rita now needed two hundred and fifty dollars, which is ten percent of the bail amount. Rita had thirty five dollars in the house and she went to Jim's boss, as he instructed her to see if he could help him with the remaining amount of bail money. His boss, with reservations, and telling her that when Jim got out he had to talk with him, gave her the money. Later that day, Jim was released and with Rita waiting for him at the jail's door, they went home. That night they rented a movie, the one that Rita picked out, and watched it.

SEPTEMBER 7 1996

I think I did the right thing. Jim is out of jail and seems sincere about not letting it happen again. He tells me that he is just very jealous. I'm really not like my mother, I never heard my father tell my mother that he loved her. I think in my case, especially with the baby coming, Jim is going to be okay.

COMMENTARY

It is hoped that an abuser, realizing that society is not going to consider spousal abuse as being just a family matter, and In addition, hopefully, hearing the clanging of the cell doors as they're closed, will cause the abuser to, if nothing else, to decide that the cost of his behavior is to high. The abuser can go back to his mate and work hard at making their relationship work. It happens, but not always. There are those that do not believe that the latter is likely. Certainly when a crime is committed by a stranger, being put through the arrest, conviction and jail, becomes more of a confrontation between the state and the batterer and to a lessening degree with the victim. Not so with a battery, on a domestic partner. In this case the abuser will eventually be released and will return to the victim. To be alone, to sleep with him and to continue to be placed in harms way. To make matters worse, the abuser does not necessarily grasp the meaning of what occurred and becomes angrier. In Jim's case what the whole experience meant was that Rita better watch her step because it was all her fault.

The baby, JJ, was born in October 1996 and throughout the winter there were many incidents of emotional abuse. Many victims of domestic violence have said that if they had a choice, they would choose a slap on their face instead of a continuous pattern of emotional abuse. This of course is a wrong mentality on the part of the victim unless the level of physical abuse is not often and not deemed to be serious (by her). This is an indication of how some victims are more concerned about their shattered dreams, their feelings of humiliation and emptiness of not being loved. The baby did in fact bring to Rita a period of calm and happiness. There were several incidents worth mentioning where Jim had become involved in confrontations with Rita's brother Mike. Jim and Rita's mother had also had episodes of verbal confrontations, with Rita's mother being the victim. In the spring of 1997, Rita became pregnant again. Their sex life was not good by any standard. It depended on how Jim treated Rita and whether or not she willingly had sex with him, mostly she didn't. Jim resorted more and more to wanting to experiment with types of sex that did not appeal to Rita. Maybe it was just that Rita needed was romance and Jim was less romantic then ever. In fact, while Rita never mentioned it, Jim wanted to force Rita, even if she consented. It was clear to her that Jim was beginning to enjoy a kind of sex act that was in fact rape. For whatever reason The quest for power and control had also manifested itself in their sex life. In April 1997, Jim has been watching television and drinking beer. He had drunk quite a bit that night and when he went to bed, he began to grab Rita but in a gentle way. That lasted for about five minutes. Jim then ordered Rita to take off her clothes. She was in the early stages of her pregnancy, with her second child she wasn't feeling to well. What she really wanted to do was sleep. Jim was kind of stern when he ordered her to take off her clothes and Rita thought that it wasn't the first time she had to make believe she was in the mood. Jim had trouble performing that night. It could have been the beers or maybe it was a reoccurring inability to achieve an erection. What helped Jim when these situations arose was a rough sex that seemed to excite him. As his fear that he would not get an erection intensified, he began to hit Rita on her face. This excited him and he quickly finished and fell asleep. Rita did not fall asleep. She took a shower knowing that Jim would not wake up. Rita felt dirty and smelled of beer. Before falling asleep, she thought about how was she going to be able to put up with this behavior for the rest of her life. Rita actually fantasized being free of Jim. She wondered if she really wanted to be free and if she did, could she.

Dec.5 1997

Jim gave me fifty dollars to go shopping for Christmas. What does he expect me to buy and for whom. If he thinks that I should spend it on him what would I be left with to buy presents for my mother, my sister Barbara, brother Mike and of course, the baby.

COMMENTARY

The Christmas season usually brings happiness to most people, but not to everyone. People that are constantly being abused either emotionally or physically, or both, worry about matters that are not part of the "goodwill towards man" feelings. Most people overspend on gifts but those that spend more then they should become compensated by the fun in gift giving and the expectation of receiving gifts that will satisfy the desire to have things that they didn't want to buy for themselves. Associated with the gift giving is the opportunity to have big fancy dinners with people you care for. Add to this the songs, the greeting cards, the Christmas trees and all the other things associated with this season "to be merry" For Rita though it is a season to worry. Will she be able to buy gifts and if so for how much and for whom? Will she be able to plan and have a special dinner. More importantly, will she be able to get by through the season without an incident of violence. Rita's mother had mentioned to her that maybe it would be nice to have dinner at her house on Christmas eve. She had suggested that her sister and brother could also be there. The mere mention of plans made Rita feel uneasy. It's a feeling that brings on hidden desires that she would be better off not having any family. Deep down inside Rita knew that those negative feelings were wrong. She couldn't shake the thought that how lucky Jim was to not have any family to worry about. Jim's father died when he was a baby. His mother lived with a man that for most of his youth he knew him as uncle Bob. Bob was a tough man that did not appear to be afraid of anyone. He was a construction worker that always seemed to have money and always seemed to be buying beers or occasional bottles of bourbon. Later, Jim realized that he wasn't uncle Bob but his mother's boyfriend. He never allowed his mother to have many friends and she was an only child. When Jim was about fifteen years old, Bob developed some kind of liver disease and died. Jim's mother appeared to have a string of boyfriends and the only memories that Jim had was that most of them abused his mother physically. She moved to another state and when Jim refused to go, he stayed behind living in a friends house. Eventually he had to leave and Jim then began to live by himself. Little by little he lost contact with his mother and rarely heard from her. Rita's perception that Jim was lucky was wrong, he secretly wished to have relatives. People usually interact with their friends and family throughout the year but at Christmas everyone felt better about everyone else, be it for religious reasons or succumbing to seasonal hype. Rita did not enjoy Christmas because she knew that she would get the jitters at the mention of plans. Even the thought of plans made Rita feel unhappy. Rita did have something this year that could change everything and that was, Jimmy Jr. or JJ as they called him. Rita found herself enjoying all of the many quite moments she spent with her baby. On Dec. 15 1997, Jim came home with a Christmas tree and told Rita that she should go and buy some decorations. Rita told Jim that she had no money and he told her to use some of the grocery money that she had stashed in a draw. There were actually two stashes, one of which could come in handy someday, maybe even save her life.

DEC 21 1997

Jim said why don't we ask my family to come over to the house on Christmas day. I held my breadth as I suggested Christian eve. I am very happy that he agreed, almost cheerfully.

Commentary

The days became weeks and the weeks turned in to months. Seasons come and seasons go. Christmas and birthdays and all the festive holiday would pass. The abuse continued but not always in a spectacular fashion. They differed only in the level and degree of pain. Not always did the physical abuse hurt more then the emotional abuse. There were times when Jim's yelling and obscene name calling hurt much more then a slap across the face. But not always. In the summer of 1998, Michael was born and with a new baby, new thoughts about how finally her life could turn around. Rita remembered how happy Jim seemed to be when he learned that she was pregnant with J.J. She remembered how at one point, after Michael's birth, how for a fleeting moment, she was going to achieve her happy life. Throughout Rita's pregnancy of Michael during the spring and summer of 1998 Jim did not seem as elated about having another baby. Not that Jim demonstrated any contempt or disapproval of the prospect of having another baby, he just seemed to be indifferent. The biggest surprise to Rita was that instead of moving closer to be a family, having two children did just the opposite. Most of the tension lately had to do with the children crying, being spoiled, misbehaving and all the other aspects of having children. To Jim it seemed as if their two bedroom apartment was not big enough. He was frustrated with what he thought was a lack of space. This feeling that he was a man living in a nursery. One night Jim had come home drunk and with his shirt stained with lipstick. Rita knew better then to ask him about it. There was that feeling, that, oh so familiar feeling, of having a broken heart. Rita could not suppress a meager desire to at least let Jim know that she wasn't totally naive. Jim take off your shirt so I can let it soak Jim had been going out a lot lately and coming home late. When Rita questioned him, it would create a reason for Jim to become violent. Rita mistakenly saw these moments as reasons, when in fact they were just events of meanness. A reason to maybe reinforce Jim's self esteem at the cost of lowering Rita's. So Jim told Rita "you want this shirt, come and get it." Rita went into the room where the kids were sleeping. J.J. had a small bed with rails along the side to prevent him from falling and the baby, Michael, was asleep in his crib, the one that used to be where J.J. slept. Rita picked up a bible that was given to her by her pastor, and started to read passages from it. Rita had been able to get permission from Jim to go to church. The pastor knew about Rita's problem's but chose not to get involved directly. He did try to help Rita by telling her to read certain passages that he said would help her. Rita needed something to believe in and much of what was said in church helped her, but not today. Jim came into the room, grabbed the bible, and threw it to the floor and said A hey bitch I thought I told you to take my shirt off. Rita did not want to awaken the children and immediately began to walk away, towards the kitchen." then Jim grabbed Rita by her hair and dragged her to their bedroom. Once in the bedroom Jim took of his shirt and grabbed Rita by her hair again, placed the shirt on her mouth and ordered Rita to eat the shirt.

"Eat it Jim" Jim yelled at Rita. Rita had no idea how violent Jim was going to be this time. She could not possibly eat the shirt, but would he stop? Jim did stop trying to force the shirt into her mouth. Now he started to take rip Rita's clothes off. what are you doing I'm going to give you a lesson on taking clothes off. And then Im going to show you the kind of man I am. This was becoming the only way that they had sex, with Jim forcing her. For a person that seemed to have an normal desire for sex, Rita found that without a loving partner, it was more hurtful then pleasure. Jim on the other hand, forgetting for the moment, other failures on his part, was setting himself up for another bout of concern about his ability to live up to what he imagined he would be if not for Rita. He had very conveniently blamed Rita for his inability to penetrate his wife and it infuriated him. It's o.k. Jim It's not your fault Rita said. It's just that you've been drinking Jim seemed to think that he had no alternative, he had to show Rita that he was the man. Jim slapped Rita twice across the face. Rita ran to the kitchen, thinking that if she appears as if she was going to call the police, maybe he would stop. She didn't really believe it, but hope manifest itself in different ways. Once in the kitchen Jim punched her a few more times on her face and arms. Rita headed for the door when suddenly Jim grabbed a knife from the utensil draw and told Rita if you open the door I'll come after you, and I'll kill you. Rita thought for a moment, a moment that lasted long enough to visualize herself dead and then as she slid down against the closed door, and thought of her motherless children. At this point, she was ready to accept what ever Jim had in store for her. Suddenly there was a knock on the door. Open the door if It's your brother or your mother I'm going to kick their ass. When Rita opened the door, she found two burley police officers standing there. What's going on here. Did he do this to you.Rita was crying, not from the blows, the pulling of her hair or any of the physical aspects of the violence, but from the way her life had just seemed to go down the drain. When a person suffers a physical trauma, a kind of numbness sets in, at least until later. But that pain in the chest that unhappiness brings starts even before the first punch and last until much later. The police were mocking Jim telling him that you're the big man that hit the little lady.Rita was not very small, maybe just a little less then average. She was somewhat over weight from the habit she had developed through the years of eating away her concerns. It didn't work and all it did was to cause Rita to put on some weight. The police did not talk much this time. One of the police officers handcuffed Jim and held his head down as he placed Jim on the back seat of the police car. Before leaving the other police officer gave Rita a flyer with information about criminal charges, where to seek help and other information concerning domestic violence advocacy groups. Many states require the police to give victims of domestic violence information about protective court orders and shelters. Usually there is a hot line number that they can call in order to learn what is available in their communities. On the way to the police station the police continued their gruff treatment of Jim. Jim did not think that he would ever be arrested again, but here he was sitting in the back of the police car having to hear the police officers challenge him to show how tough he was. They joked about putting him in a cell with someone who's mother had been beaten to death by her husband. While considered tough cops they still behaved as they had been trained. Using procedures that were being implemented in most states. These procedures call for the police not to view the problem as if it were a family matter, to make an arrest if there were probable cause and to arrest the primary aggressor if there was evidence that both parties had been violent with each other. Some communities have victims advocates as part of the police department. The victims advocates, and there called by different names in the various communities, follow through after the police officers leave with information about where to acquire assistance. Sometimes if nothing else, they stay with the victim and give her moral support. When Jim arrived at the police station, he suddenly remembered what he disliked the most about being in jail. Jim did not like the smell of cleaning chemicals that were so common in correctional facilities. Jim did not like the clanging sound of the cell doors closing, and the constant murmur of voices that sometimes became very loud. The loud voices sometimes belonged to inmates, usually making some kind of demands. I want to talk to my lawyer.I want something to eat. Did my wife call? It went on all the time. It got to the point that even while hearing it, you didn't understand anything unless it rose above a murmur. Intertwined with the inmates words there was the constant murmur of the correctional officers who would spend their time talking to each other in a low voice, reading and answering the telephone after what seemed to be hundreds of rings. Their voices were usually heard when they raised it to yell at some inmate. What Jim disliked the most was having to be in a holding cell with a bunch of other guys, each one putting on an act of "tough guy" as a form of protection. It was a lot easier to impress Rita, he didn't have to act with her. With Rita he only had to hit her or otherwise just intimidate her. Encouraged by what she read on the flyer the police officer gave her, Rita decided that enough was enough. Knowing that Jim would not be released until morning Rita called her mother and told her what happened. Do you think I could come over with the kids. Rita's mother Margaret told Rita that if she could possibly find somewhere else it would be better. Remember what happened the last time, Jim got out and came here, and he will do it again. but I'm not going to go back with him this time Rita said. Finally Rita's mother agreed that if she didn't do something, now that he was out of the house, and in jail, she would not get another opportunity, at least for now. Conditions at her mother's house were not good. Their were only two bedrooms and the second bedroom was occupied by Rita's brother, Michael, his girlfriend and their three children. This was an arrangement that could not last for any length of time. But on this night Rita fell asleep exhausted from talking to her mother about what to do. She felt somewhat encouraged about going to the courthouse to get an order that would keep Jim away from her. The information she was given by the police was very clear that there was help for her.

The type of victim that has suffered ongoing abuse over a period of time will not often be able, without help, to absorb the various options available to her. The lack of friends to have for support and advise is often missing from their lives due to the way that the abuser never allows her to build a circle of friends. After taking care of her children, seeing to Jim=s needs Rita did not have a lot of time to plot and plan. She tried to maintain a relationship with her mother, sister and brother. It wasn't easy, there was always Jim to worry about, he didn't like her to be any closer to her family then was necessary or tolerable by him. Plotting and planning brought fear into her heart, so she avoided planning what she could do about her situation that would not cause her to suffer a severe beating.

Nov. 2 1998

Dear diary, I feel as if I'm a passenger on a train that only goes where Jim wants. On this train I can only look out the window to others who's lives appear to be happier then mine. There is no escaping Jim when he decides to abuse me whether it be physical, emotional, sexual or even if it means hurting the children who are also captive on this train. This imaginary train does make a lot of stops, but when I look out the window I don't see anyone on the platform. Tomorrow though I'm getting off the train. Maybe I'll find someone on the platform that will help me.

COMMENTARY

The last thing Rita thought before falling asleep was "god I hope I know what I'm doing." The next morning Rita, taking her secret stash of money, enough for a bus that left her close to an office in the courthouse that was listed in the flyer. How communities handle assistance to victims of domestic violence varies somewhat. In Rita's case she would have to speak to a person that would help her acquire an order from a judge prohibiting Jim from having any contact with her or her family. Rita walked up to the window where she was given a form to fill out. The nervousness of what she was doing made her so exhausted that she saw her own handwriting as scribbling. When she was called into the office she sat with someone that asked her to tell her everything that was going on. At first Rita didn't want to say anything. In fact she couldn't believe her own ears when she heard herself say that nothing had happened. Later as she began to feel more relaxed, the flood gates opened. All the information was put into a computer and after a while, an official looking petition for an injunction for protection (restraining order) was printed. From all she had been given to read and from all that she heard from her counselor, she began to understand that for every dilemma or problem there was always someone to help. There are many entities both public and private that offer support for those that need help. A community's level of civility can be measured by how much it helps the plight of those of us that are in need. In Rita's case it was how to find a way out of this relationship that she was beginning to understand could harm her and her children. She thought someday I'm going to help woman that find themselves in a predicament like the one I'm in. After talking at length with the counselor and talking about how to maintain herself safe, Rita left for her mother's house. But mom if I go back with Jim he's going to hurt me. And if you stay here he's going to show up and get into fight with your brother Mike, besides there is really not enough room here. Margaret, really did not want to relive her own abused life at the hands of someone like Jim and had no stomach for any confrontations with Jim. Not to mention that her son mike was at the house with his girlfriend and kids. Eventually Rita's mother told Rita to stay in the living room until she found another place.

Nov. 5 1998

when I get my diary that I have hidden at the house I'll include what I'm writing on this note pad. But for now my dear diary I need to clear my thoughts. Tomorrow I need to call the counselor to tell him that I wrong about having a place to stay, maybe he can help me. I also have what seems to be a million questions about how to get my life started. Where will I live? Where will I get money? More importantly, how will my kids eat?

COMMENTARY

The next morning Rita called the counselor at the Domestic Violence Intake Unit. In some communities their called advocates, or some other similar title. Sometimes the office listed is called The Woman's Shelter. Rita told the intake person about her mother's advise to go back with Jim and how crowded it was at her mother's house. The counselor made arrangements for Rita to go to a shelter. Rita called the shelter as she was told to do by the counselor. When she gave her name, the person on the telephone arranged to meet Rita at location close to her house. The shelters policy was not to go directly to the victims house just in case the abuser was in the area. They did not want Jim to know where the shelter was. Sometimes a person who is arrested is released from custody before anyone has a chance to get away. About an hour later Rita was at the front entrance and when she heard the driver speaking into an intercom, in order to have someone press a button and have the automatic door open, allowing the car to enter. She had this sinking feeling that the shelter was going to be like a prison. Once inside, Rita's children were given toys to play with in an adjoining room while Rita spoke to a social worker who filled out some forms. The social worker was a kindly person who by the way she spoke gave the impression that she knew what emotional pain was. Her name was Joan. Joan was never a battered spouse, in fact she was happily married. Joan simply felt good about helping people when they were in need of help. Joan majored in psychology, had several cats, cared about the environment and was a consummate writer for federal grants that enabled her to get funding for a never ending need for food, clothes and other emergency needs. Joan and Rita spoke for a while and Joan gave Rita the shelter's rules. Also Rita was given a list of chores that she would have to participate in doing,along with the other woman. There were one hundred and twenty four woman at the shelter at that time. The shelter had a capacity for one hundred and thirty eight woman. More then half of the woman had children and there was additional room for about fifty children up to sixteen or seventeen years of age. When older children were involved, or when the victim was a man, arrangements had to made to have them stay at certain hotels. These were of course not great hotels to say the least. There was also the constant battle with budgetary restraints. The battle lines in the war against domestic violence are drawn with the courts on one end and the shelters on the other. In between we have law enforcement which tries to rescue those that are in immediate danger. Gavin de Becker, in his book "The gift of fear" writes that America has tens of thousands of suicide prevention centers, but no homicide prevention centers he goes on to say that the closest thing to a homicide prevention center are the women's shelters. Joan took Rita around to the various rooms and introduced Rita to the other woman. Some were tending to their children others finishing up their chores and others were watching the television in the recreation room. The shelter resembled a hotel of sorts, without carpeting or televisions in every room. Rita noticed that the rooms were quite nice. Her room had a bed for her children and a slightly larger one for her. There were also a couple of dressers where clothes could be stored. Victims are advised to take certain steps prior to actually leaving an abusive relationship, and one of those steps is to have some clothes hidden somewhere so that several change of clothes is available at a moments notice. Also the victim should put away an amount of money. Money that could be used for a hotel, but at the very least, money for transportation and food. If the abused woman is an alien, she should have all her immigration documents. The list of safety tips adds other essentials like an extra set of keys for the house and the car. Abusers will invariably take the keys to the car in order to prevent the victim from being able to move around. Also prescription medicine and the medicine itself. It is also recommended that if the victim has a close nearby friend, she should establish a kind of code that will signal the friend to call the police, in what could be a life saving action.

November 8 1998

I have been here for three days. My children are happy oblivious of the trauma that I have been experiencing lately. They have toys to play with and other children to play with. Playing with other children is kind of new to them. We have food even though we don=t always like what the other mother=s make. One thing for sure is that we all are learning about each others cultures in this very diversified environment. I=m really nervous about the hearing that is schedule for November 20. Everyone tells me that it will be absolutely safe. Another thing that is for sure is that while this place is a little better then I thought it would be, I really miss my home.

Commentary

When it comes to missing her home, De Decker goes on to say in his book, that a victim becomes addicted to the feeling of relief when the violence ends and what Rita may be feeling is really a subconscious desire to get a "fix" of a false feeling of well being brought about by the highs and lows of cycles of extreme fear and extreme relief that she is safe now.

On the morning of the hearing, called the permanent hearing, the Judge will determine certain issues that could not have been addressed at the time of the petition for an temporary restraining order. On this date the Judge will decide if the restraining order that was issued temporarily should be extended and for how long. This court order if granted is called a permanent restraining order. The judge will also determine when and how the abuser can see his children. Also the judge can order the abuser to pay child support and to attend a kind of anger control class. Many abusers are also sent for an evaluation to determine whether or not the abuser is dependent on liquor or drugs. In some cases the judge will also determine that the children should go to a children's center where they can obtain therapy to help them through all the violence they witnessed.

Certainly not all respondents in restraining order petitions are abusers and without a doubt all the petitioners are not always victims, but in this case Rita was a victim and Jim was an abuser.

The case for false accusations has judicial merit but the Judge would determine the veracity of the allegations. The number of which is not close to the types violence and subsequent harm that occurs in this narrative. Such is Rita's case.

Rita sat in what at this courthouse was called the victims waiting area. Some feel that it is not politically correct to call the victims, "victim," but instead we should call them survivors, this may be so but in this case the political correctness did not extend to calling the victims waiting area, the petitioner's waiting area or the survivor's waiting area. This should not distract from Rita's story who sat waiting for her name to be called. She wondered as she looked around and wondered where Jim was. Rita tried to find Jim among the prisoners that arrived at the courthouse accompanied by correction officers's These men, there were five of the Respondents who were handcuffed and had been arrested previously for battery and were responding to the subsequent temporary restraining orders that had been granted to their victims. In this case, those that had not been released, who were still in the custody of the Correction Officers would still be handcuffed until brought into the courtroom. It should be mentioned that they are not called Defendants because these proceeding are not criminal but Civil. Criminal charges would be addressed in another Court. Today's hearings were, as mentioned earlier, were to determine if the restraining order should be granted, and for a longer, indefinite period of time. Rita did not see Jim among the prisoners. Wasn't Jim being held until his arraignment? The arraignment would be when the charges against Jim would be official and his opportunity to plead his guilt or innocence. At his bond hearing an amount of bail was set, but Jim would not be able to pay and would remain in custody at least until his arraignment. Sometimes a prisoner is released with a stay-away order but the Judge refused and Jim remained in custody. Jim's public defender assured Jim that when the time came, he would make a plea for Jim to be released and that a date would be set for a jail report. An arrangement was actually arrived to before the trial date. Jim was released a day before the hearing. The State objected to the public defenders motion to release Jim, but the judge agreed with the defense pleading to be able to work. A date was set for a jail report and Jim was released. Jim hoped that if he could only talk to Rita he could get her to drop the charges. In most states the state or district attorney's office can proceed with the criminal case, with or without the victims desire to continue the prosecution process. Very often though, without the victims cooperation, the prosecution either plea bargains or diminishes the charges. About an hour after sitting down to wait, Rita needed to go to the ladies room. Rita would also check on her children who were at a nursery. Rita was lucky enough to live in a community where the court had a facility where the children could be taken to while their mother's (or father's) could attend the hearings. Rita did not know though that Jim had left the waiting area where he had been asked to sit and where he was not permitted to have contact with Rita. He had watched as Rita got up and began to walk along the corridor towards the ladies room. As Rita entered the ladies room she thought that she saw someone that looked like Jim. The person disappeared behind a wall. Rita thought no I'm beginning to imagine things, they assured me that I would not have any face to face contact with him. Rita left the ladies room very unsure of herself and began to walk to the elevator. Jim, like many abusers, have uncanny intelligence to find ways to outwit the person that they have chosen as their life-long victim. Jim learned that sometimes parents take their children to the child care center on the fourteenth floor. He wasn't sure if Rita was with the children and waited for her to come out of the ladies room. Rita began to walk, not to the courtroom, but towards the elevator. Jim positioned himself near the elevator but somewhat out of sight. Rita waited by the elevator door. The light was already on as someone had called for the elevator before her. Rita was apprehensive as she waited. She faced the yet unopened door as Jim maneuvered himself just behind Rita. When the door opened about ten people went in and began to push the buttons to their respective floors. Rita also went in and so did Jim. After pushing the button for the fourteenth floor, where the nursery was she stepped back to not block the elevator door. Rita turned white when she saw Jim standing next to her. Rita froze not knowing whether to scream, or run, if she could. Rita actually found that she was unable to speak from the fear and shock of being in the same elevator with Jim. Everything seemed surreal to her. The colors of the walls seemed brighter and the floor seemed to waver. Rita was having the same sensations that one would have if they were suffering a panic attack up to and including shortness of breadth. The door opened several times. "Should I get off, what if he gets off with me, and there's no one around." The same kinds of fears that she had always felt about leaving Jim. It was kind of like that imaginary train pulling into a station and finding no one on the platform, only worse, because on this train, the elevator, was real and it was really happening. The door opened, she did not hear the recorded voice instructing elevator passengers to be careful getting of the elevator. Rita took two steps and felt Jim's hand hold her arm. I just want to talk to you, I'm not going to hurt you. Look Rita, if you continue with this process, I won't be able to see the kids. Rita managed to tell Jim that your not supposed to talk to me or be near me. I know but I just want you to do what's right maybe if we could be together again I will be able to take care of you and the kids like I'm supposed to. "You know that I can't afford to pay for rent and food and all of that and still be able to give you money for you and the kids if I'm still in jail." "Besides you know that I love you and I can't live without you." "If you could just give me one more chance you'll see that everything will be all right." Rita was becoming more confused and her will to resist was draining. Jim then interjected a little threat as if the script called for it by saying if I can't live without you, I'll kill myself and if I'm going to die, I might as well end it for all of us. Rita had heard about men who in their obsession did in fact kill their children. The victims advocate that I spoke to told me that it wouldn't be necessarily up to me and that only the Judge could dismiss the case. The fact is that Joan was right. If the judge wanted to, he could enter a permanent restraining order, whether she wanted it or not. "But if you tell the judge that the kids miss me and that you know that I will never harm you again, and that you need and love me, he would, in the best interest of the kids agree with you." Jim told Rita to sound convincing as to the Children needing him. Sometimes when there is a report of child abuse just the opposite occurs. Usually when a report is made to the Department of Children and Families about possible child abuse. They often insist that the mother seek a restraining order to keep the abuser away from the children. In this case no one made any report that the children were being abused. The children were certainly being abused. They were witnessing the constant abuse. They were aware that their father battered their mother. They heard her crying and also they felt the pangs of hopelessness their mother felt.

"Look you can't stay with your mother, it's too crowded there, and anyway I'm going to prove to you that everything is going to be alright.

"Look I'll wait for you to see the kids and then we can go back to the courtroom and see what happens." Rita was with the children for no more then five minutes. She found them playing with toys and very content to be with other children and with the very nice ladies who were taking care of them. When Jim and Rita reached the courtroom door Rita went quietly to where she was supposed to have been sitting. Rita was immediately approached by the bailiff. "where were you, They called your name and I told the Judge that you were here, that you might have gone to the bathroom." yes I did. "Well okay they will call you again, right after this case." Rita began to listen to the bailiff announce the return of the judge who had taken a recess. The honorable Judge Spencer J. Madison, now presiding, all stand. The Judge walked behind the bench and sat down. Please be seated. After everyone sat down the Judge asked if the next party was ready. "Both are present, judge. The bailiff then announced the name of Rita Evans. Rita was directed to a seat behind a table on the right side of the courtroom. Jim was then told by the bailiff to sit behind the table on the left. If any of the parties had been represented by counsel, they would have sat at the table with their respective clients. There were some attorneys sitting around, some were listening to the proceedings in anticipation of when their clients were called. Others were outside talking to their clients. The courtroom was abuzz with activity. There were various clerks sitting near the front of the courtroom near the judge. Some of them were whispering about things that probably had nothing to do about any case in particular, but with one ear on the judge. In what would have been the jury area was being used to sit the several men who were responding to the petitions for permanent restraining orders. Rounding out the rest of the people in the courtroom were two or three correction officers and an interpreter who would be used if any of the parties involved could not speak English. One of the clerks walked up to the bench, placed a blue folder and whispered the names to the judge. The judge took a few minutes to read the allegations. Mr Jim Dempsey it is alleged that you battered Mrs. Evans and then chased her into the kitchen where you then grabbed a kitchen knife and threatened her. " What do you have to say for yourself" said the judge.

"Well your honor if you ask my wife she will tell you that most of what was said was exaggerated." What was said, was said, in the heat of an argument, Jim stated.The judge asked Jim if he had grabbed a knife." No your honor, I did not" "what about hitting Rita with your fist" "judge, a few days earlier Rita had bumped her head on the car door when she was getting in.Jim thought that it would be unwise to say that Rita had admitted to the police that she had hit herself. The judge glanced at the police arrest report, which the police called the form. There was no mention of the police actually seeing a knife or even witnessing the incident. The photographs that were taken of Rita's bruises were still with the police or the State attorney's office waiting to be used in the criminal battery case that had not yet materialized. The police in fact had not been summoned to appear in court. Cases that have to do with restraining orders are not criminal cases and are treated differently than criminals cases. In criminal cases, there are attorneys or public defenders who's sole purpose is to get their client off by having the case dismissed or otherwise have the court find the defendant not guilty. When that's not possible, they attempt to get the case dismissed by some legal procedure. Finally, if all else fails, he would attempt to get the best deal or the shortest sentence for his client, the defendant. The prosecutors do exactly the opposite. In a civil case such as the one that is being heard at this time, no one has been charged with a crime so there is no need for a public defender or a prosecutor. When one or both parties have attorneys representing them, it's usually to get the better of decisions concerning whether or not the restraining order should be kept in place, and if so, the respondent's attorneys attempts to get the best deal for child support and visitation if there are children involved. The judge returned his attention to the paperwork in front of him and began to read the narrative of her allegations She had taken an oath after reading the narrative attesting to its truth and correctness. Let's see your husband came home, you questioned him as to where he had been and he than dragged you into the bedroom by pulling your hair. The judge looked directly at Rita when he gave this very concise version of what had occurred. Rita began to cry.

"Your honor I exaggerated a little, I don't want to continue this, what I would like is for Jim to come home to me and the kid's. The Judge looked down at the paper and then sternly looked back at Rita. "But he also forced you to have sex and he also threatened you with a knife

"As I was saying, I said a lot of bad things to the Police Officers to and I didn't say anything about a knife, I don't know where that came from. "Well you know that your under oath, and you know that you read the statement before signing off on it." Rita started crying again and pleaded with the judge to please let Jim come home. The Judge looked at Jim and asked him if he had something to say. Jim turned on his best behavior and told the judge that he had learned his lesson. Jim told the judge how he always supported his family and that without him they would suffer. Actually it appeared that with him they also suffered. Jim told the judge that the violence was a thing of the past and that he gave his word that it would not happen again. After hearing both parties, and Rita's pleading to please allow Jim to go home with his wife, the told them both that he did not have to dismiss the case but that he would decide what to do after Rita had an opportunity to talk to the counselor that assisted her in the first place. The judge instructed the parties to wait in a separate areas and that he was going to send for someone to talk to Rita. One of the clerks called the intake office that luckily was in the same building and told the counselor that the judge had requested that he go to the courtroom. The counselor went immediately to the courtroom and approached the bench. The judge explained that the petitioner had requested that he vacate the temporary restraining order and not issue a permanent restraining order. The judge asked counselor to talk to Rita to see if he thought she was asking for the dismissal out of fear. The counselor that helped her was summoned and while the judge put aside this case, Rita waited for the counselor in another area. Jim was not allowed to approach Rita. A few minutes later the counselor arrived and he and Rita went to a designated area to talk.

"Hi Rita, I understand you want to have the restraining order dismissed"

"Look I really need for my husband to come back, and if he can't, he won't be able to take care of me and the kids." "He promised me that he would never hit me again"

"Did he intimidate you into saying these things, you know that I've heard this many times before."

The counselor and Rita spoke for about an hour. Throughout the conversation Rita kept giving reasons why she no longer was afraid. Whenever she was confronted with an opinion that she might be placing herself in danger, she would throw logic to the wind and insist that the restraining order be dismissed. Eventually, the counselor wrote a memo to the Judge indicating that she was adamant about allowing Jim to return. The counselor also documented what had been said during their conversation. The counselor also indicated that she appeared to panic at the thought of not dismissing the restraining order. Later, when the Judge faced both Jim and Rita in the courtroom he gave Jim a stern warning about what could happen to him if he ever was abusive towards Rita again. The Judge understanding the dynamics of what was happening, and feeling that Rita was probably going to continue to have contact with Jim even if the restraining order was kept in force, dismissed it with prejudice. This meant that he retained jurisdiction in matters concerning this case. Also, the judge reminded Jim that he still had to face the criminal charges and that the court would monitor him as part of his release conditions.

November 28 1998

I think I did the right thing, at least I hope so. We had a Thanksgiving dinner at my house and my family came over. We had a wonderful time. Jim even allowed me to invite the pastor from my church and two of my church friends. In fact I think that I may have solved all of my problems.

COMMENTARY

Rita could very well have solved her problems, if she had, this story would end right here. Jim did behave himself insofar as hitting Rita was concerned but he did get verbally abusive towards her at times. On Rita's part this was a tremendous trade off, verbal abuse instead of hitting, pushing or pulling hair. "Everyone suffers verbal abuse, right?" She asked herself. As far as Jim was concerned all he had to do was to administer a degree of intimidation, without hitting her, to vent out his frustration that he felt. The frustrations with always wondering if this good behavior of his,so he thought, was going to eventually cause him to lose power and control over Rita.He feeling fatigued at his attempt and was causing a rising level of tension. Was the honeymoon phase about to end?

DECEMBER 5 1998

I'm noticing a change in Jim. He seems to be getting angry more often.

DECEMBER 10 1998

Today Jim and I went Christmas shopping. We bought presents for the kids and for my mother. Jim even suggested that we buy presents for my Brother's kids. It looks like It's going to be a nice Christmas after all. "It's funny how I keep hearing that song in my mind," *it's beginning to look a lot like Christmas."* I don't remember ever being so happy."

COMMENTARY

Rita's perception that she was never so happy was genuine but flawed. Rita's emotional life was like a see saw. At times she felt very happy but was this just an example of experiencing a "fix" from feeling a lack of despair. The rest of the Christmas season went about as well as it ever did for Rita. On Christmas Eve Jim, Rita and the kids went to her mother's house. They had a nice family Christmas dinner. Rita's brother Mike was there with his Girlfriend and their kids. Rita did all she could do to prevent Jim from drinking too much, without him noticing it. The hours flew by and at midnight they all opened their presents. At first Jim wanted to not give the kids their presents until the morning. Jim wanted the children to find them under the tree. The children, knowing that Rita had taken the presents to her mother's house "by mistake," begged their father to allow them to open their presents at midnight. Jim became the instant hero when he said that it would be alright to open them up. Jim had a rush of importance, a feeling of being so in charge that his saying that it was okay made everybody happy. Jim, Rita and the children got home at about two in the morning, and they all went to bed and fell asleep rather quickly. Very early in the morning Jim woke up and began to fondle Rita. Rita was feeling happy at the days events and had a feeling of peace. They made love as they hadn't in a long time. Rita was not feeling fear throughout their love making as she had on almost every other occasion in the past. For the first time in a long time she was a willing participant. Her thoughts were that they could be happy if she worked at making it that way. The next day Jim watched a lot of television. Their children played with the toys that were given to them. The children pretty much ignored the clothes that Rita had bought for them, as kids their age usually do. Even though Rita had told them that they were from Santa Clause, they still preferred to play with the toy metal trucks that Rita's mother gave them. Rita's brother's girlfriend also bought Rita's children some toys that they discarded for the moment only to return to them later. Rita could almost sense, but not quite, that a certain rhythm had changed in the cycle of violence wheel. That would just go to show that the phases of the cycle, while predictable in general, could not be counted on to hold any set time table. The rest of the week went fairly well. Jim showed that he was upset a few times, only as if to remind Rita that things could change quickly. Jim had no idea how quickly things can change. A few days after New Years day, when Jim arrived at his job, his Boss told him to go to his office, that he needed to talk to him. There was no place to sit, the only chair was behind the desk where his boss sat. Nothing matched in this furniture store office. It seemed as if the furniture in the office was left over, unclaimed or damaged furniture. Papers were thrown about and it had the appearance of a kind of stock room rather then an office. When Jim=s boss came in he got to the point very quickly.

"Jim. Things haven't been going too well around here lately"

"my wife's son from her Ex, lost his job and I have to give him a job"

Jim was shocked. "I've been with you for four years, And now that I have a wife and two kid's your going to dump me"

"look Jim, he's not any good for sales, and neither are you." "He's not good at furniture restoration, in case something breaks, and neither are you." Jim's Boss tried to soften the blow by appearing to be in a bind. "You known that if he doesn't workout, I would have to support him anyway." Jim didn't even contemplate for a second that pleading would make any difference, and became aggressive in his demand for whatever money was owed him. Jim's Boss told Jim that his Stepson was already on the road making deliveries and that he could go home. Jim's Boss told him that he would send him a check. Jim said that he was not going to leave without his money. They argued for a while. Eventually Jim got his money and left. Getting the money took some of the edge off of Jim's anger. When Jim got home, he arrived with a six pack of beer. Jim told Rita what had happened, with a spin towards he being the one that was not going to put up with the Owner's Stepson working there. He told Rita that he was sure that he would find a better job right away. After a while, Jim decided to not continue the conversation. Maybe he was afraid that he was going to mix up his lies with what he thought was the truth. Rita knowingly did not push for more conversation and accepted his statements about getting another job quickly. Rita thought more about how bad it would be when she ran out of all of the money she had, which at the moment did not exceed forty dollars. She knew that one trip to the supermarket would feed the family for a week at best and that then the rent, electricity and telephone would be due. Jim on the other hand ended up drinking four of the six beers, ate dinner, watched a basketball game and went to sleep without incident. It occurred to Rita that maybe the social worker that she spoke to, and been so helpful at the battered woman's shelter, could help her. When Joan answered the telephone, she remembered Rita right away. The social worker at the shelter got so into their clients lives that they usually remembered them as one remembers family or at the least, close friends.

"How are you Rita, I hope that this is not a call about what I fear the most." Joan had misgivings about having said that because she did not want to victimize the victim, or hopefully in this case, the survivor any further. Joan followed immediately with "Don't worry what ever it is we can overcome it." Rita told Joan that she had been doing okay, and that she had gone back with Jim, and that she had no complaints about his treatment of her. Rita had not told Joan everything and Joan had not thought that she did. After answering the standard questions about how were the kids, Rita told her about how Jim lost his job. I was worried about the normal things that someone in my position would worry about but I'm also worried about how Jim will behave if he doesn't find a job right away. Rita was right it was an additional worry. Rita had learned about the dynamics of domestic violence from her own experiences. Joan asked Rita if she had told Jim that she was going to talk with her. Furthering her knowledge about how things work Rita replied "no, heavens no, I told him that I was going to talk to someone about getting a kind of emergency help."

Most of the help I could get you, I could get you if you were here and you know to come here you need to actually be in imminent danger, we are after all a shelter for battered women. Rita started to say something but was interrupted by Joan, "but until, and if you needed to come to us, let me see what I can do for you.

I think Rita said, that what I need is help to get me through this period of time that I don't have money to feed my family."Well I want you to call and make an appointment with the Department of Children and Families." Joan gave Rita several telephone numbers and told her to call. Many of the same agencies that the shelter for battered women use, are the same that other agencies, such as the red cross, homeless shelters, and many other groups who's purpose is to help people who are in an emergency. Many of these organizations are faith based. Joan did not at this time think of Rita as victim but as a survivor, she was wrong. The next day Rita told Jim that she had to go to see about getting food stamps and money to help pay for their utilities. Jim told Rita that he was going to apply for unemployment insurance. All in all a sense of relief settled in with Rita and Jim. The following week Jim went to pick up his check, others would be mailed to him if needed. At the unemployment office they gave Jim a check and gave him two referrals for job interviews. So ended a week that could have exploded in violence but thanks to Rita's efforts and guile and Jim's perception that his sudden bad luck was going to be very temporary helped. Jim went to his first interview and really liked the company. The job was delivering food supplies to big restaurants and large hotels. Jim was exhausted from filling out the employment application and the actual interview. When he was told that they would let him know he didn't go to the other interview. Several days later he received a letter thanking him for applying but told him in a very polite way that he did not get the job. Jim began to use a lot of the little money that they had on beer. Several weeks went by and while they had the food stamps to help with the food bills, the rest of the bills became a burden. They were running short of money whenever they needed to pay the rent. The idea that Rita could find a job was full of peril. Rita knew that depending on how Jim viewed his wife as the person who would support their family could be dangerous. Jim might view Rita working as a sort of a diminished power. If that were the case he could certainly revert to his violent ways. Rita suggested that if she could temporarily get a job, they would not feel the pinch of being harassed by bill collectors. She also emphasized that he could with the extra money buy gasoline for his truck and anything else he needed. Surprisingly, Jim allowed Rita to find a job, reluctantly agreeing to take the kids to a day care center. Secretly, Jim liked the idea to, at least, temporally, be free to do what ever he wanted during the day. When Rita announced that she was hired by a large discount buying club Jim made sure that Rita knew that she was not capable of getting a normal job that required a smart women. It was his intention to make sure that Rita did not think of herself as being someone that could survive on her own. Jim was playing a mind game with himself. Rita was realizing more and more that she could handle working and be able to continue her housework. Things were somewhat better then they expected, mostly due to the employee discounts that they got from the store. That enabled them to buy clothes for their children, and themselves. Jim did set the ground rules. Jim said that he would take Rita to work and then take the kids to the daycare. As soon as Rita got her first paycheck, Jim insisted that they go together to cash the check. Rita did not protest even though what she wanted to do was deposit the money into the bank and then pay their bills with checks. Rita figured that it was better to leave well enough alone. Jim of course availed himself of enough money to allow him to buy beer. The pattern that ensued was that Jim would drink during the day and greeted Rita fairly drunk. Naturally he didn't allow her to drive even to pick up J.J. and baby Michael. Rita had experienced verbal abuse but Jim had not been physical towards her in weeks, until she told Jim that he could have an accident if he drank to much and get arrested for driving drunk or worse, have an accident with the kids in the truck. Are you telling me what to do? Jim snapped from the driver's seat as he sped away from the daycare's driveway. As soon as he drove a few yards, he slapped Rita across her face. "You told me that you would never hit me again" Rita said crying.

"I wouldn't if you would only not be so stupid." When they got home, Rita said nothing and started preparing dinner. When Rita began to serve the food Jim told Rita that if she served him that slop, he was going to throw the food in her face. Fortunately Jim was not hungry, drank a beer and went to bed. Rita fed the children, put the kids to bed, took a shower and went to bed. As she had expected Jim needed a jolt of power and that would come from his demand for sex. Jim did not take a bath, smelled of beer and forced Rita to partake in a very rough sex. Jim forced Rita to do things that she did not want to do. She did all she could to not throw up her dinner, a dinner she ate unhappily. Jim fell asleep but Rita stayed awake for hours worried that the promise, Jim's promises, of a happy life together would unravel. Jim was drinking heavily on a continuous basis and continued to be verbally abusive. He continued with his foul language directed towards Rita. As the days went by Jim appeared to Rita as if he hated her and the kids. Never in their relationship did Jim's emotional abuse reach these levels. Rita wondered how long she was going to be able to stand what to her was a torture possibly worst then being hit across the face. The next day she would find out.

On January 26 1999, Jim did not come home. Rita wasn't really concerned with whether or not Jim was alright. If anything she was concerned that if and when he came home, he could possibly infect her with something. Rita thought God knows what he's doing and with whom. Jim had gone to a bar where he knew he'd find old friends, some of which were there as they had always been. They talked and complained about just about everything as they drank beers. Jim had a few dollars that Rita gave him and when that ran out they used the remaining money that his friends had. One of Jim's friends suggested that with the remaining five dollars they go to the liquor store and buy a bottle of cheap wine. They didn't have a big selection it was between a wine called thunderbird and another called golden spur. They chose golden spur because it was a little bigger. They all went to a park that was nearby and continued to drink, passing the bottle back and forth between the three drinking buddies. Maybe because Jim had not eaten or because he had been mixing beer and wine, Jim became more intoxicated and began to make nonsensical remarks about how it was Rita's fault that he lost his job and how she had caused him to be arrested. Jim remarked that he was going to straighten out Rita when he got home. His friend encouraged Jim telling him that it's a man's job to keep his wife from disrespecting him. One of three men passed out and the other said he was going to the place where he slept. Being homeless he slept behind a loading dock in a desolate part of the neighborhood near the railroad tracks. Jim decided to head home.

Rita had spent the day hoping that he did not come home and as she cleaned the house and picked up after their kids she sensed that feeling of imminent danger. She spent the day feeling nervous and unhappy, trying to build courage so that if and when he returned, she would be able to face him and do whatever she had to do. After dinner Rita and the kids went to watch television. Rita started to watch a program that had to do with home decorating and Michael and J.J. became restless and went to their toy box under the bed. J.J. found a broken fire engine and began to fantasize going to tall burning building which was actually the leg of the kitchen table. Michael found a police car. J.J. liked the police car better and abandoned his fire engine and took the police car. Michael started to cry. Rita's nerves were on edge and she got up screaming at the kids. She took away the toys and made them go to bed. Rita shut the television and began to cry. She was at the end of her rope and thought how much better it would be if she were dead. At this point Rita thought that even Jim's cruelty could not make her feel any worse then she felt at that moment. Rita then thought that maybe she could feel better if she wrote into her dairy. She once had the thought that writing in her dairy was like praying and she needed to pray. It was also like talking to herself, and she sure felt as if she needed to talk.

JANUARY 26 1999

Dear diary I had some terrible thoughts about dying and how it would be better, but that's not how I really feel. I have my beautiful kids to think about and somehow I feel that for them there will be a great and beautiful life ahead. I just would like to be normal, to have Jim become a normal husband and father, if only it could be.

COMMENTARY

Rita's despair turned into a momentary feeling of fatalism. She felt better when she began to put her thoughts on paper but passiveness about matters that had to do with family, her kids, her life and Jim crept into her thoughts Rita remembered that Joan, the social worker had told her to call her if she ever needed to talk. Rita hesitated for a moment and then dialed the shelter's telephone number.

"Hello can I help you." The person that answered the telephone did not want to identify where the person had called. Lately there had been a rash of calls from abusers who found the number and wanted to speak to their wives or girlfriends. Maybe not to just talk but to attempt to continue to intimidate or threaten them even as the victim was trying to hide from the abuser.

This is Rita Evens, I'd like to speak to Joan. "Joan left about two hours ago, and she left complaining that she spends to much time here." Rita kind of understood that maybe she should not have called so late, it was about nine p.m. "Okay I'll call her some other time." At this point, Rita was beginning to feel very alone and anxious. She toyed with the idea of paging her, she did mention to call her if she wanted to talk and gave her, her pager number. Joan answered her pager within ten minutes. "Hello this Joan, can I help you." "Joan, this is Rita, can I talk to you." Rita immediately thought that she should not have called and told Joan that she realizes that it was late and that she would call her tomorrow. Joan explained that her pager is used for emergencies and that it was no problem. The first thing that Joan wanted to know was whether or not this was an emergency. Rita said no, but that she felt that soon he was going to hurt her. When Rita began to talk about how she felt that she hoped that Jim never came home, It made Joan feel as though finally Rita was ready to leave him. Joan became especially concerned when Rita began to tell her about those very negative thoughts she had about wishing that she were dead. Rita and Joan spoke on the telephone for about an hour. Joan's lifestyle had been forged many years ago even before she graduated from college. Joan had been an intern during her senior year before graduating with a degree in psychology. Joan had also minored in criminal justice. Usually people like Joan could work somewhere else and possibly make more money. Instead she chose a career at helping others. As did others who dedicate their lives in assisting those less fortunate. Joan did not hang up the telephone until she was convinced that Rita was not about to do something rash.Joan also convinced Rita that if Jim did anything, even so much as make a vague threat, she should again be granted a restraining order and get him out of her life forever. Rita was getting her clothes ready for tomorrow when Jim staggered up the stairs and began to fumble for his keys. After realizing that he had left his keys in his truck he thought that he would get them tomorrow. Jim banged on the door hard enough to make Rita feel as though her worst fears would come true about his becoming physically violent. It was that sane old pattern. The pressure had been building and that false honeymoon period was a long forgotten time. As soon as Jim walked in Jim told Rita that it was her fault that he had left his keys in his truck because of those fuckin locks you always use.

"Everybody locks the doors, especially when they're alone with young kids." Rita said. Are you going to start answering me back again.

Have you forgotten what happens if you disrespect me. Rita started to say that she had not disrespected him as she changed her mind about explaining anything to him, she felt the first slap on her face. Rita thought that as long as the children didn't wake up she would except it.. Just then she felt a second slap. Rita tried to run into the bedroom when Jim grabbed her by the hair. The thoughts went racing through her head. Could I have out of the room? Do I calm him down. I know that none of this works. "You bastard I'll show you who the boss is around here." Jim's was yelling at Rita with a very slurred speech, completely drunk.

"Please Jim don't hit me anymore." Rita heard the kids crying in the next room, too frightened to come out. Jim continued to call Rita every dirty word that he could think of as he continued to hit her. Maybe it was to a degree because he was drunk, but mostly it was his hatred for Rita, a hatred that surfaced because of his own behavioral traits, that he opened the kitchen drawer that had the spoons, forks and knives. At this point, he felt that, in his demented manner, that if he meekly closed the drawer, he would be viewed by Rita as being weak. So Jim grabbed a kitchen knife and told Rita that she was a bitch and that she would pay. "No Jim don't, for the sake of the children, please don't." Police officers Rodriguez and Sullivan were just paying for their dinner at a cafeteria near by when they heard the dispatcher. "Unit 3654 QSK." "This is unit 3654, QSK." responded Officer Rodriguez. "We have a report of a domestic violence problem." "Any weapons involved, QSK." The dispatcher said "No none that caller mentioned." "A neighbor saw a man running and getting into a pick up truck after hearing a lot of noise, QSK. Police officer Sullivan told the dispatcher that he and officer Rodriguez were on their way. The police car's arrival attracted a group of people. When the police officer got out of the car he asked someone if he knew anything. Most of the bystanders seemed anxious to make comments, but none really knew anything besides hearing the commotion. As the two police officers entered the building. The police officers approached the door to Jim and Rita's apartment with caution as their experience dictated. When they heard whimpering and children crying they tried the door, which opened easily. Once inside, they saw Rita on the kitchen floor moaning but conscious. The children at the sight of the police officers came out of the room and ran to their mother who immediately hugged the kids and began to cry. Officer Rodriguez saw blood on Rita clothing and began to ask her what had happened. Officer Sullivan went back to the door to prevent any onlookers into the house. Officer Rodriguez called the dispatcher and told them that they needed an ambulance and that the perpetrator had left about twenty minutes ago. The dispatcher then asked other units to be on the look out (bolo) for a man who was described as about five foot ten, medium build, and driving a white pick up truck. Other police officers arrived within minutes. One officer, Officer Jones took the children into the bedroom and attempted to calm them down as she also wrote into her notebook whatever JJ told her for future reference or to possibly be used for prosecution purposes. Officer Jones called the dispatcher and asked to have someone from the Department of Children and Families to come to the scene to take the children to a children's shelter because it was clear to the paramedics, who had just arrived, would be taking Rita to the hospital. Rita was talking between sobs and moans telling the police that she needed to call her mother. Police officer Jones asked Rita if the children could stay with her mother. Rita told Officer Jones that she wanted only her mother to take her kids. Officer Jones called the dispatcher and told her that they would not need the investigator from the, DCF as they were commonly called. Officer Jones said that she would be in contact with the investigator to let him know the exact address of where the children would be. The paramedics were busy examining Rita while officer Sullivan talked to the dispatcher calling in additional information concerning Jim and the make, model and color of his pick up truck. Rita's mother Margaret, arrived at the Johnson Memorial Medical Center, emergency room. The emergency room was much more than a room, as the sign inside the lobby stated, it was more like a suite. The receptionist was on the telephone when Margaret approached but sensed the urgency on her face and hung up. The receptionist was accustomed to people asking for information and appearing desperate to know where someone may have been taken. The receptionist asked Margaret for the name of the patient and after Margaret told her Rita's full name she started to look at he computer screen. Margaret, her son Michael his wife Kim and their four kids crowded around the reception desk as the receptionist typed in more information, finally looking up and telling Margaret that there was no one by that name on her list of patients being treated in the emergency ward. Margaret nervously told the receptionist that the police had called her and told her that they were going to take her to Johnson Memorial. The young lady told Margaret that she may have been brought in within the last hour or so and that maybe her information had not been put into the computer yet. "I need to see my daughter, she's been stabbed and I have no idea how bad it is." "Look, don't all of you go into the nurse's station just down the hall but if you go, ask at the desk maybe they can help you."

"Michael stay with Kim and the kids and I'll come back out as soon as I find out something." Margaret practically ran to the nurse's station and waited for someone to at least acknowledge that she was standing there. There was a lot of activity, not all seemingly important. The nurse's station is like a big office crammed into a small space. There was one older man going about his housekeeping duties, moving the wheeled cart from one area to another. At each area he tied the plastic garbage bag with a wire tie, placed the filled bag into yet a larger bin and then replaced it with a new garbage bag that he put into the trash bin under the desk. There were other bins, some with symbols that looked frightening, that were used for medical trash that apparently he was not going to be taking care of at this time. Two doctors were talking in a stern manner apparently about a patient as they both read from a chart of some kind. Several nurses were going back and forth to the patient's rooms and one, who may not have been a nurse, was talking on the telephone, probably with a relative, seemed annoyed. Rita could not really tell what color uniform belonged to a nurse or to an assistant nurse or even a doctor. She pretty much would have assumed that the ones with the stethoscopes were the doctors. On this day she didn't much care and just wanted to find out where Rita was. "Excuse me, can I ask you something?"

One nurse stopped reading what seemed to be information or instructions about what a certain patient was supposed to have and asked Margaret what she could do for her. "I'm looking for my daughter, she should have been brought in within the last hour or so. she came in an ambulance."

"Hold on, what's her name and what happened to her." Margaret responded that her name is Rita Evans And she was stabbed.Oh okay, someone was brought in about thirty-five minutes ago and she was taken into a treatment area back in the trauma center. If you go back to the waiting area where you were, I'll get word to you. As Margaret began to walk back she heard the nurse ask someone on the telephone about a patient who was a stab victim, and after listening to the other person, she told the other person that the victim's mother was in the waiting area. Margaret felt a lot of remorse because she felt that she could have done more for Rita. She couldn't get rid of a the feeling that she was responsible for all that has happened to her daughter. Feeling responsible is something that Margaret was used to from years of being in the same situation as that Rita had found herself in. While Margaret was not at this time being abused, she still had some of the traits that had been instilled into her during a lifetime of being made to feel as though she was incompetent and worthless. So she sat, walked and sat again. A female Police Officer brought Michael and J.J. to her. About three hours later a Doctor with a surgical mask still on around his neck came out to the waiting area and asked, looking in the direction of Margaret who was Rita's mother. The Doctor had experienced going out into the waiting area and looking for the most worried of people milling about. He seemed to know instinctively who was Rita's mother. "Mrs. Evans, I'm Doctor Rosen." Even before Margaret could get a word out the doctor said "first let me tell you that your daughter is going to be alright, she's a pretty lucky woman. The knife entered her body at just above the ilium, that's the wide bone that forms the hip. It actually nicked the bone" "The knife apparently was not pushed with enough force to go in as far as it could have" The doctor went on to explain that a small hole was made in Rita's upper digestive tract and that did not cause a great deal of internal bleeding as had been their initial concern. "Rita is asleep and will be sleeping for a while. She was awake when she was taken to the recovery room and was given a sedative. "She did ask for you and wanted to know how her children were." "You can stay and wait or come back in the morning." The doctor told Margaret that he would be making his rounds at about eight in the morning and that he would be able to tell her more then. The children were restless and Margaret decided to go home. Her son Michael was tired from working all day and fatigued from all the worries and running around. "I just pulled on to third street and I think I'm right behind the pickup truck that we're looking for, QSK." Said the Police Officer.

it's a white 1987 ford pickup, we don't have a plate number yet QSK."

Jim saw the police car close behind him and noticed the police officer talking into his radio. I hope he turns off and if he stops me, I hope I did something wrong he thought. But he didn't remember running any lights. Just then the lights on the police car lit and started flashing. The reflection of the red and blue lights off the interior of Jim's truck scared Jim. He pulled over and as the police officer stopped his car behind his truck. Jim he began to plan what he would say. Jim didn't need to plan or say much because as soon as Jim asked what's wrong officer he noticed that the police officer had his hand close to his weapon. "Sir get out of the vehicle and don't let me lose sight of your hands." As Jim got out of the car he asked the police officer what was wrong, clinging to a little hope that this was a traffic stop. That hope disappeared as soon as the police officer told Jim to place his hands on the top of the trucks top. The officer frisked Jim and asked him if he had anything in his pockets that might hurt him. Jim replied that he did not. Maybe to show Jim that he was in charge and to put Jim in a more difficult position to make any quick movements, the officer kicked Jim legs lightly outward. As two other police cars pulled up, the officer began to handcuff Jim. Jim made a feeble attempt at appearing puzzled. The officer had Jim's wallet in his hand and began to ask Jim questions that he already knew such as his name and where he lived. He asked Jim where he was going and where he had been. Jim said that he was going to the store to buy cigarettes. The officer told Jim that he must have passed hundreds of stores considering where he lived. The police officer began to recite Jim's Miranda rights as the other officers looked with their flashlights under and over the truck seats. All of the police officers knew who Jim was and what had happened and at this point, without telling Jim much, they went about looking for the knife, or anything else that might be in plain sight. By now there were five police carat the scene and a crowd of onlookers that had gathered. Sargent Holmes told the police officer that stopped Jim, Officer John Amat, to take Jim to the station. Officer Amat held Jim's head down as he placed Jim into the back of the police car. The officer drove to the police station and within minutes the police and the onlookers were gone. Officer Amat pulled up to a parking space reserved for official business, in this case bringing Jim into the police station to begin the booking process. To Jim he was reacting to each step along the way and fearfully wondering what was next. To the police officers placing Jim into a holding cell was considered one small step in a long process involving law enforcement, Corrections, Prosecution and the Judiciary. Officer Amat held the handcuffed Jim Evans by his arm firmly. He held him at arms length and quickly pressed the buttons of the door lock release. It was the only door that was not operated by the officers identification card. The door led to a kind of lobby, separated from the main entrance and the "Sergeant's desk" usually manned by two officers, not always a sergeant, by a partition with large windows. Officer Amat waved at one of the officers through the window. Officer Amat opened two more doors and entered an area with large cells. Without saying a word an older officer opened a cell door and placed Jim inside. Once in, Jim was directed to back up and stick his wrist through a slit in the wall of bars. The handcuffs removed, Jim eyeballed the three other men being held, and sat down on a long metal bench. Jim hated the coldness of everything. The air conditioner was always at it's coldest setting, not for the prisoners, but for the comfort of the corrections officers. Most of the items in the cell were made of stainless steel and were always cold to the touch. Jim Laid back, the back of his head touching the cold hard bench and eventually fell asleep. Jim had felt very fatigued from worry and a lack of sleep.

Rita open her eyes and saw her children standing by the bed. The nurse had bent the rules and allowed the children to see their mother. Mostly they were allowing the children to go to their mother's bedside for her sake. Margaret told Rita that because the kids were there, she would have to leave to take them to Michael and then return. After talking about the assurances that they both got from the doctors and nursing staff that she would be alright, the conversation shifted to Jim. Margaret told Rita that A detective Markham had called her to check on the kids and to tell her that Jim had been apprehended. Rita felt nothing at the news that Jim was in jail. Oddly enough what she wanted to do at the moment was to make an entry in her dairy that Jim was in jail and that she did not care one way or another. There were some thoughts that Rita did not allow to surface completely about what will happen when Jim is released again. Throughout the conversation that Rita and her mother had, both little Michael and JJ. Laid on the side of the bed and hugged Rita. Just as Margaret began to gather the children to leave, the telephone on the side of the bed rang. Rita had too many tubes hooked up to her arm and one to her nose to be able to reach for the telephone. Margaret answered and told Rita that it was Joan from the shelter. Rita asked to put the telephone receiver on the pillow so that she could talk to Joan. When she began to talk she stopped and told her mother that it was alright to leave that when it came time to hang-up she would ask the nurse to help her.

"Okay I'll be back tomorrow." After thinking for a moment Margaret told Rita that it was strange how things turned out. "It's okay Mom I would be very surprised if things had turned out any different, I'll see you tomorrow, I love you. I love you too.

"Hi Rita, when I heard what happened I couldn't help thinking that I could have prevented it from happening." "No you shouldn't think that way, In fact I think that what you always tried to tell me about that I was not to blame for Jim's actions, is true." "I know that he's in jail right now and he would have a hell of a time convincing me that it was my fault." Rita and Joan spoke like old friends which they had become. Joan told Rita that if there were anything that she could do for her to just tell her. As Rita began to hang up she remembered something.

"Hello Joan, are you still there." "Hello Rita I'm still here, what can I do for you." "I just remembered something, your going to come and see me right." "Sure I am." replied Joan. "Well can you go by my house and tell my mother that I need my reading glasses and then look under a lot of junk in the top drawer of my dresser for a diary." Joan told Rita that sure she would and I promised that she wouldn't read anything written in it. "It's okay. I know you understand and you know that I use it as therapy." Rita and Joan said goodbyes and Rita called for the nurse to tell her that she was feeling a lot of pain. The nurse came back with a cup containing a pill and a cup of water. "Here take this it will help you go to sleep and you will feel better in the morning." Rita drifted off to sleep with the knowledge that she would get better and very importantly, a new understanding of what had happened to her and how she didn't have to let it happen. Rita was a bit surprised as she fell asleep that she did not feel depressed or frightened.

Jim felt a great deal of depression as he sat on his steel bench hoping that he could get sleepy. As Jim slid down to lie down he felt very cold. He put his arms inside his shirt to keep warm. The night was horrible with the depression that Jim felt and the cold that seemed to reach his bones. Jim also was bothered by not knowing what the police knew. It was obvious to Jim that they knew that he had stabbed Rita but somehow he thought he could come up with an excuse. Around three o clock in the morning it occurred to Jim that if for some reason Rita had died from what he did, he would be facing murder charges. Not knowing what he faced kept Jim from getting any worthwhile sleep until at about six o clock in the morning when a frenzy of activity began among the Correctional Officers, some getting ready to leave and a trickle of Officers coming in. Those that entered the cell area all walked in with a coffee and some kind of pastry. Jim wanted a cup of hot coffee in the worst way, if just to make himself warmer. Jim knew that if he asked about getting coffee or something it would just empower the guards to act as they were keepers in a zoo. Jim remembered how it was the last time he was in jail, there was never a time when he could get someone to be kind to him. It seemed as if the officers enjoyed making life miserable. Jim thought that why could they not be reasonable as Rita used to be. He knew that if he were home, Rita would have served him a cup of coffee or anything else he wanted.

If Rita is okay. Maybe I can talk to her and see if she can help me Jim thought. Jim started to talk to the other three inmates that were in the cell with him. It was that same old jockeying for your corner of the cell. The same old act of trying to show the other guys that you were tough. And the carefully chosen words as to not let on that you were afraid. No matter what was said the common thread was that everything that happened was someone else's fault. At about nine a.m. the guards came up to the cell bars and told each inmate to back up to the space in the bars and to stick their hands through it. They were each handcuffed one by one and to each other then led down a corridor to an elevator. Not to anyone's surprise they did not use the elevator, they were led down two flights of stairs. Within minutes they were placed in another cell to wait for the bond hearing. "Okay, lets go guys, hands through the bars."

The corrections officer looked like a football player who had put on a corrections uniform. There were three other officers but most of the prisoners attention was on the way the shirt sleeve appeared to be biting into the big guys forearms. Jim and the four others were led through what appeared to be a maze of doors and hallways until suddenly they were in a large room with a television camera and a large monitor. All of the prisoners had their handcuffs removed and were told to sit. One of the officers told them that when their name was called, he should go to a podium where the Judge would be talking to him. The officer told them that there would be public defenders on the left and prosecutors on the right. Before he was finished talking the officer had to lower the volume on his radio. "4123 this is 7856 we're ready to start." Several names were called before Jim's was called. Some had lawyers in the courtroom. The set up was such that the Judge could see the defendant on his monitor and the and the defendant could see the Judge. Everyone in the Courtroom could see both on several large split screen televisions.

"James Evans, case number 99-31255, aggravated battery, assault with a deadly weapon and attempted murder" announced the Bailiff. The judge appeared to be tired, having addressed the cases of about thirty inmates to see if there had been probable cause for an arrest and then to establish bond if any. "There seems to be probable cause, what does the state say." "The state is asking that the defendant be held without bail." The public Defender immediately asked that the a reduced bail be ordered, suggesting to the judge that the victim was out of danger and that there was no fear of flight. The judge had no desire to entertain a bunch of young attorneys trying to make a name for themselves, if only to impress their superiors. The judge read the arrest form and then studied Jim's criminal record. "The defendant will be held without bail, the case will be set for arraignment.

Jim was led away. Those that would be getting out soon, as Jim once was, were led to another area. Jim and five other inmates were taken through a maze of passages and placed in a cell that held the five of them. Soon they would be taken out of the courtroom and taken to the county jail. The arraignment was set for February 12 and Jim knew he would be there at least until then.

COMMENTARY

While Rita recovered at the hospital Jim awaited for his arraignment. Jim did not fool himself into thinking that he could call Rita for help again to try to get his charges reduced so that the Judge could set a reasonable bail. No point in thinking that Rita would help him with somehow getting bail money, if ordered, or at least possibly the ten percent the bondsman got for putting up the money. Jim felt very depressed and did not participate in the idle banter that the others conducted for the entire time that they were together in that cell. Jim was transferred to the county jail and placed in a cell with three others. The cell appeared to be designed for inmates that were going to stay for a while longer. The cell had a toilet and a sink, made of what looked to be of stainless steel, and four bunks two on each side. While some cells actually had a television set, Jim had to watch a television that was on a shelf that was mounted on the far wall. Jim had to watch from between the bars.

FEBRUARY 2 1999

I don't think that Joan read any of my entries into this diary. I'm sure glad she brought it because like I once wrote, writing in my diary is like talking to myself in a kind of sane way.

FEBRUARY 10 1999

Whenever the phone rang I would get frightened but now it's not happening as much. I guess because my mother answers the telephone I don't get a chance to let Jim scare me. I'm getting used to the idea that what Jim wants is not so terribly important to me anymore. I'm feeling better and the nurse told me that the doctor said that I could begin to walk to the kitchen and to the bathroom by myself. The pain is gone but at night when I remember what happened in the kitchen the day that Jim stabbed me, I shudder at the thought of how frightened I was. Sometimes remembering is just like it's happening again, thoughts are really things.

COMMENTARY

Rita's situation started to become routine. The bandages covering the stab wound was the only outward sign of what happened to Rita. Rita was eventually allowed to go home. Rita was pretty much taking care of herself. Her mother was tending to the kids most of the time. Rita spent a lot of time reading magazines and watching television. Jim had not been able to circumvent Rita's mother when ever he called from the jail. When Rita's mother complained about Jim's telephone calls, the assistant state attorney told the Jail guards to tell Jim that his telephone privileges would be taken away if he called Rita. Jim complied because knew that he needed on occasion to call his lawyer and really needed to know that he wasn't totally cut off from the outside world. He didn't realize that he would always be able to talked to his Defense Lawyer.

So Jim stopped calling Rita but didn't stop hating her. He still thought that all his current problems were her fault. During the following week Jim's Defense Attorney had been talking to the Prosecutor assigned to the case. He was a 32 years old assistant state attorney who had been hired by the District Attorney's Office about two years ago, about two years after his passing the bar exam. Upon passing the bar exam, he worked for a reputable if not prominent criminal lawyer. He had decided to be a prosecutor while he was sill in law school and impressed the supervisor of the Major Crimes Division. Now with two years experience with the State Attorney's Office, handling mostly contempt, probation violation and simple battery cases, he now had his first felony case. At first he thought he had an attempted murder case but with the help of his supervisor the charge was reduced to aggravated battery. Still a felony, but the sentence would be a lot less hard time. Jim's defense lawyer was able to bargain for dropping all other charges and charging Jim with aggravated battery. Jim would have to serve a mandatory three years and then be on probation for two additional years. Jim's lawyers convinced Jim that he could get out of jail sooner if he stayed out of trouble in prison. He pointed out to Jim that he was going to get credit time served which counts all the time that Jim had been incarcerated.

Then with good behavior maybe Jim would be out in about eighteen months.

February 27 1999

I'm feeling much better. Soon I'll be able to go back to work. I think they will take me back at the discount warehouse. As for Jim, I feel as though I finally have him out of my system. Looking back I think that I never really loved him. What I loved was a dream, a fantasy about how my life should or could have been. But most of all I lived a mistake. While I knew that he was not what I wanted, I feared him, and the fear covered any rational thinking on my part.

COMMENTARY

Rita did get her job back and her mother took care of her two children along with her brother's kids. With the money that her brother gave her mother, they were relatively happy. It showed because Rita seemed to be getting prettier. I fact Paul, one of the stockmen was constantly saying nice things about how she looked. During March of 1999, their schedule was the same and and they usually ate lunch together. "Hey Paul, what are those books that you always seem to have in your locker, the ones you don't seem to read anymore." Paul laughed. "Yes it's your fault that I have fallen behind with my school work." "Your going to school?" "I go to school at night, I'm studying computer programming, no actually It's a technical course that doesn't require a four year degree."

Rita told Paul that she was sorry that she made fun of him not reading. "No I was only kidding" Paul said. "I have been reading at night when I'm at home. "How is it not my fault that you don't read during your lunch anymore. Actually." "I wouldn't call its fault, I like talking to you."

Rita and Paul spoke to each other during lunch and they played those word games that people play. In this case it was a romantically good way to play. Not that Rita was even remotely desirous of a romantic relationship. As time went by Rita and Paul got to know a lot about each other. What Rita liked about Paul was that he was funny and made her laugh all the time, not with actual jokes but with everyday humor. The one thing that Paul did not know about Rita, was all her troubles in the past with Jim. Paul had nothing to hide. Rita knew that Paul lived with his mother and father. He was an only son. He seemed to have confidence in his ability to work for a company in their computer department and make a good income. Paul was convinced that some day every company would be completely computerized, requiring people like him to solve problems that employees have with their computer's throughout the day. Paul told his father that he really did not think that he was cut out for college and that what he wanted to do, would not take him too long to get into the field. He was right. In early April 1999, Paul was accepted for employment with a state agency. Rita could not help feel Paul's joy and enthusiasm. He now set his goals on eventually moving up to programming.

APRIL 9 1999

I am so happy for Paul, but I'm going to miss him. I wonder if he has given any thought to the fact that we won't have each others company anymore.

C<small>OMMENTARY</small>

Hey Paul, you only have a week to go, said Rita. "I know Paul said as he opened the bag that contained his sandwiches. "Do you make your sandwiches or does your more them" Rita knew that Paul lived with his parents and thought that Paul came from a normal family. Paul was the only child and lived with his mother and father. It seemed to Paul that his safety and security was the norm and it never occurred to him that was any other lifestyle. Rita did not tell Paul all the details about her dysfunctional past. Paul and Rita spoke a lot during their lunches together. Do you get tired of the sandwiches or does your mother ever make you something special. Paul explained to Rita that very often his mother would pack leftovers from the previous night's dinner. Paul had to sometimes insist that all he wanted was a sandwich.

"She thinks that I'm to skinny and is always trying to fatten me up" Paul said. Rita told him that he looked just fine the way he was, as she thought to her self that Paul in fact had a very nice body. Paul suddenly told Rita that if she wanted to taste his mother's good cooking she should come over one day and have dinner with him. Rita thought that it was the first time that Paul said something to her that was sort of personal and serious. Up to now their conversations were filled with humorous stories and those word games that people play, sometimes saying one thing and meaning something else. Rita just as suddenly surprised herself with her desire to tell Paul that she would love to meet his mom and Dad. It might mean that they could continue being friends and see each other even after Paul goes to his new job. Rita had some misgivings and thought that maybe she should not even think of seeing anyone, not even Paul in a romantic way. Was going to Paul's house a kind of declaration that they were a thing, at least while she was at his house, and is that what his parents would assume.?

"Okay when do you want to come over, you know that Friday is my last day today is Tuesday already"

Very cautiously Rita told Paul that they could talk about it later in the week. Rita worked the rest of the day second guessing herself as to what she should have said about Paul's invitation. There was a lot of conflicting thoughts about where this was headed. Was she ready to even think about someone? Was she reading more into Paul's invitation than it deserved? "Hey Paul you must invite all the girls you know to dinner. I bet your mother is tired of cooking for all your invitees" "Yeah sure, you'll be the eighth dinner guess I'll have this week, someone is going to have to double up with someone else" Paul said laughing. Rita saw Paul once more before leaving for home and waved at him. On the way home Rita was trying to analyze her feelings and not being able to come to any conclusions she decided to just enjoy what ever she was feeling because it felt good. The fact that it was a "good" feeling was totally foreign to her.

APRIL 21 1999

Dear diary, I'm so confused. While I thought that my life with Jim was all I was ever going to know, I'm realizing that there is still hope that I can be a normal woman even with some rough spots but that I can experience happiness. There seems to be a big difference between hoping for a moment of happiness, but fearing that it will only last for a short while and expecting happiness, and believing that it will last. Do I owe this to Paul? My mother said that I should give life a chance. To let life give me what it will give me and that as long as it's good, accept it.

APRIL 22 1999

Tomorrow I'm going to agree to have dinner with Paul at his home. What if he doesn't ask me again or doesn't even bring up the subject?

COMMENTARY

Rita was anxious for lunch to arrive and when it did, she sat and waited for Paul to show up. He didn't and Rita felt a sadness come over her. It was the first time that she began to realize that she had been falling in love with him. Or maybe it was just disappointment in not seeing Paul at lunch. She kept thinking that she was stupid for not taking advantage of his invitation right away.

There is always a fear that when you care about someone, the person being cared for doesn't reciprocate. In Rita's case her lack of confidence accented these fears. Rita kept saying to herself, "stupid " "stupid " Rita had no way of knowing at the time that Paul had to go to a pre-employment medical check up and drug test, which he passed with no problem. The next day she went to work feeling down until she saw Paul driving a forklift truck. Rita waved at him and he immediately stopped and walked to where Rita was making believe that she was buying a soda from a vending machine. The company they worked for was easy going and not to strict about employees talking to each other. Rita's boss was a nice guy who was satisfied as long as the employees did their work. Even so, Rita didn't want to abuse her status as a good worker and did not want to be obvious about her wanting to see if Paul had come to work that day. Paul smiled at Rita and asked her if she missed him. Rita thought that maybe he was playing with her. Paul dispelled any negative thoughts by not waiting for Rita to answer by saying that he missed her. I was waiting for you at lunch. "I had to go for a medical prior to starting work next week"

"How did it go" she asked? Oh everything is fine except that I forgot to mention it to you the other day In fact Paul added, "I realized yesterday that I have no way of contacting you."

"Well why don't I give you my phone number." "Sure I'll see you at lunch, give it to me then." Later when they were having lunch, Rita gave Paul her telephone number and told him to call her anytime he wanted to. Paul put the napkin she wrote her telephone number on and put it in his pocket and said "but what if you decide to take me up on my invitation: how would you get in touch with me if you ever decide?" "I think you should give me your number if it's alright with you" Rita was surprised herself at her boldness when she then told Paul "but I already decided" She told Paul that She would be happy to have dinner with him and his family. Rita said and was not about to blow this opportunity. Paul and Rita having exchanged telephone numbers continued talking but before they went back to work they agreed that Friday he would pick her up at about seven o'clock and take her to his house where his mother would have a nice dinner prepared. Finally Rita gave Paul her address and they parted. Rita's heart was racing unlike anything she had experienced with Jim.

April 24 1999

I don't know.

1. Will Paul change once he feels he doesn't' have to hide his true personality?
2. Am I making a bigger deal about Paul then it deserves. And finally,
3. Can I know when I can go back to allowing someone into my life again. My mom says that I should just watch Paul's actions and try to determine if he is for real and that if he shows any sign of being abusive, drop him.

COMMENTARY

Someone who has gone through what Rita has gone through would naturally have a lot of baggage but the human experience always mitigates how well we remember all the unhappy experiences. This allows us to go on with life after an unpleasant situation. It helps us in getting back up after a fall and gets us back into seeking fulfillment in life.

Rita did not forget what happened to her but the rough edges sort of faded and gave her hope that she once again could allow herself to become involved in a romantic relationship. Rita though, was a lot wiser about what she would get into. She would continue cautiously, but what she really wanted was to go headlong into being in love. Rita's mother Margaret was right about letting Paul's actions show the truth about what kind of man he was. In Paul's case it seemed obvious that he was who he showed himself to be, but of course, maybe not. Men who are abusive towards their mates usually cannot hide their abusive characteristics for very long. If abusive individuals are given enough time they cannot help to be themselves because if they attempted to hide their abusive behavior they would soon become overwhelmed by the effort. On the other hand someone who effortlessly behaves in a way that is tolerant and concerned about someone else's feelings does not need to disguise himself in an attempt to fool someone into accepting him into their lives. Paul was a well adjusted man who reflected the tranquility that exemplified his family. His family while small was part of a larger family that included cousins, uncles and aunt's. Paul's life was relatively normal in that he had experienced both positive and negative incidents in his social life. His last relationship ended with Paul feeling depressed because it was his girlfriend who left him for someone else. As it turned out it was for the better because as it seemed, his girlfriend was attracted to a kind of man that was overly assertive towards woman. The last Paul heard was that she was being abused by her new boyfriend. Paul had overcome any unhappiness and was not scarred from the experience.

APRIL 27 1999

I only have a few minutes to write a few lines, Paul should be here soon. Paul made feel a lot calmer about going to his house, even before going on a regular date. I hope I look alright I didn't have a lot of time to get ready after work. I think I hear him coming.

COMMENTARY

Paul arrived at Rita's house and spoke to Rita's mother for a while. Rita's Mother was impressed with how well spoken he was. Paul told Margaret about his new job and how it was going to be the start of a rewarding career. Rita introduced Paul to her children J.J. and Michael and he generated a friendliness that the kids picked up on. Fortunately children can recover from traumatic experiences quicker than adults because it seems as though their minds are fertile to new ideas and experiences. While it's true that a young mind can be stigmatized and have an effect on their future behavior and well being, new positive experiences can alter the harm done. After some small talk with Rita's mother and her kids, Paul and Rita left.

The fact that Rita had children was a constant worry for her. She did not know what Paul thought about the fact that she had children. It wasn't that she hadn't mentioned that she had been in a relationship with someone else, but she talked about her past life with Jim and her kids only at the beginning of their friendship and then hardly mentioned anything about them since. When Paul said that her children seemed well adjusted Rita took the opportunity to say that if they seemed well adjusted it was in spite of a not so well adjusted relationship. The problems that she had with Jim could, she thought, ruin something good even before it started. Paul was true to the impression he generated by opening the door to his car to let Rita in. When they arrived at his house, Rita felt like a school girl on her first date. There were those gnawing thoughts about her background that kept surfacing. She couldn't help wondering what Paul's parents would think of their son seeing someone who had living with someone and had had children with him. It appeared to Rita as if Paul's parents expected more from their son.

"Hi mom I want you meet Rita, she's the girl I was telling you about" "Hello Rita, I'm Gale, I'm glad you could come" "Fred, Paul's father is in his room, he'll be out in a second" Gale asked Rita to sit and make herself comfortable. Rita was given a choice of things to drink and excepted a cup of wine. Rita really did not drink very much but it seemed so appropriate to sip wine while they talked. It also might have the effect of calming her a little. A little later Paul's father Fred walked into the living room and introducing himself. After just a few minutes it became apparent to Rita that Paul had gotten his sense of humor from Fred and that made Rita feel very comfortable. "Paul tells me that you have two kids" Fred said. It seemed as if was asking a question but it also seemed to Rita as a way to get her to talk a little about her personal life. It did not surprise her that Paul's parents would want to know as much as they could about someone that their son knew and liked her enough to bring her to his house. Rita described her children to Fred and Gale, but stayed away from any mention of Jim.

The dinner was delicious and the talk at the tables delightful. Rita felt as if this was the first times she had ever talked to such caring people. Most of their conversation was about about Paul. They spoke about Paul's youth and how he never had been in any trouble. If they only knew that her children's father was in prison as they spoke. The evening went by rather quickly for Rita. It seemed to Rita that it went by quickly because it went well. After dinner they sat in the living room and spoke while the television was on. It seemed that everybody's television stayed on while people socialized. It was about 11 o'clock when Rita mentioned to Paul that it was getting late and that maybe she should be going. Paul told his mother that he was going to take Rita home. Rita thanked Gale and Fred for a wonderful dinner and she was happy to have met them. Their satisfaction with meeting Rita seemed genuine. In the car Paul told Rita that his parents seemed to like her even before she asked. "I know when my parents like someone" Paul said. "I'm happy that they do, that is if in fact they really do" Rita replied. When they arrived at Rita's house Paul told Rita that he had a great time and asked Rita if it would be alright if he called on her again. Rita feeling very good about herself told Paul that he should do it soon because she was going to miss talking to him at work.

"I'm going to want to know more about how your doing with your new job.

Paul opened his door to get out of his car, in order to go around to open the door on Rita's side, when suddenly, after opening the door he held Rita's hand and actually gave her hand a light kiss while saying goodnight. It seemed to Rita as if she was dreaming about being a princess and Paul was a knight in shinning armor. When Rita opened her house door, she found Margaret awake watching television. Rita and her mother spoke for about two hours and it took Rita about another hour to relax enough to go to bed and to sleep.

May 27 1999

I was looking forward to writing in my dairy because I want to see what I'm thinking about my visit to Paul's house. It was a wonderful day. I'm a little worried about being happy but I have been happy before. I'm not going to write what I had written in the past when I when I started the dairy. At that time I though I was happy and wasn't. But of course I'm not going to spoil how I feel with negative thoughts. Tomorrow I'm going to call Joan at the shelter.

COMMENTARY

"hello, can I speak to Joan Bernstein" Rita asked. She had an emergency and had to leave, she's at the hospital" The receptionist had second thoughts about telling the person on the phone where Joan was. First Rita told her she was a friend and a past victim of domestic violence and had stayed there for a time. The receptionist corrected Rita and told her that the politically correct way of referring to herself now was as a survivor. Rita thought that it didn't change anything insofar as to what happened to her, call it by any name it was abuse and of course being stabbed for sure. Rita asked the receptionist if Joan would be back to the shelter. The receptionist said that didn't know but that she said that she would call to get any messages.

"So could you tell her that Rita called and could she please call me back, she has my number"

Rita had called from her workplace during her morning break and found the warehouse gloomy without the expectation of having lunch with Paul. Rita had been planning for days how to find a way that she could receive personal telephone calls when she wasn't at home and decided to get a cellphone. She would get one after work. The real reason was to make herself more accessible at all times in case Paul called. She found a place that had a deal for a cellphone that was only $25 dollars a month, but there was a only small amount of calls that she could make with no free weekends. Rita knew that she would have to limit her calls to 100 minutes a month or pay extra. If she didn't use all the minutes she could roll them over to the next month. After work she got the phone and made her first call to the shelter. She asked the receptionist to give Joan her new telephone number. "I'll give her the number but she just walked in a few minutes ago" "Okay, great, do you think I can talk to her" Rita said. Within minutes Joan got on the telephone and greeted Rita. "Hi Rita how are you?" I'm fine" Rita said and added that she needed to talk to her. Joan asked Rita if she was okay. Joan was apprehensive about these phone calls. Calls like these from past victims were sometimes bad news. Rita told Joan that she had met someone. Joan was somewhat startled by the news. Very often victims of domestic violence gravitate right back to the same abuser or another one just like him. Joan did not think that Jim had been released from prison yet, even though it would not come as a shock if he had. Joan told Rita that they should have a nice long talk and they agreed to meet at a fast food restaurant in a shopping center that they both knew. Joan did not tell Rita that the woman who she had gone to the hospital to see had died and that her killer was the victims third abusive boyfriend since her first encounter at the shelter about four years ago. "Hi Rita, you been here long?" Rita told Joan that she's glad that she arrived because she's starved watching others eating. they ordered their lunch took it to a table and began to immmediatly talk about Jim and how he came close to messing up Rita's indeed coming close to ending her life. Eventually Joan asked Rita what she had on her mind. Rita told Joan all about Paul and how she felt about him. She also told Rita about fears that she could or might be getting into another abusive relationship. Joan explained to Rita that in the most likelihood she was not necessarily choosing another abusive man, but that it did occur that sometimes woman go right back into another abusive relationship. With many victims the very emotions that caused them to allow their previous circumstances also caused them repeat the same mistake. That was a real concern for Joan. "If your questioning your feelings I would think that you are probably safe" Joan said. Rita told Joan all about Paul's family and his background and how different it was from Jim's. "I really think that Paul is actually how he appears to be" Rita told Joan. "Let me ask you if that at this point could walk away from Paul without being feeling hurt" Joan asked. Rita asked Joan if she thought that Rita could not pick a man that could be nice to her. No I think that if you were to see a sign, any sign, you re capable of walking away. Rita explained that she felt strongly about what she learned throughout her terrible experience with Jim and that she had gotten over those hidden desires to be taken care of. Furthermore she felt that she was thinking clearly about what to expect. Joan asked her why than did she call. Rita told Joan that she respected her opinion, and knew that she cared for her and would help her decide things. "you've been a lot of help to me, Joan." "But you know what? I'm going to do exactly as you say" Rita told Joan that at the first sign she that noticed that she was getting into something similar to her time with Jim, she would bite the bullet and leave Paul, before it was too late. Rita and Joan finished their lunch. They had a lot of laughs and Joan mentioned that Rita looked genuinely happy. Joan also, maybe as a way to leave Rita with a somber thought, told Rita she was so happy to have seen her again, but that she felt terrible about having experienced the tragedy of the death of someone she tried to help in the past.Rita understood what Joan was saying and let it sink in. Rita and Joan parted and Rita went straight home to think and see what she was going to say in her diary.

April 28 1999

Yesterday I spoke to Joan to get her opinion and together with my own thoughts I think that I'm going to allow myself to enjoy my feelings for Paul and enjoy the way he outwardly shows how he seems to care for me, more and more as time goes by. my mother and brother are also feeling as if he's a nice guy.

Commentary

The friendship slowly became more than a casual friendship. Going out to dinner and sometimes to the movies became an on going activity. On many occasions especially on weekends they both went to places where they would go as a family. J.J and Michael quickly forgot the trauma that they experienced. It really wasn't forgotten, it was placed in the back of their minds. Children, fortunately can restore a level of rehabilitation that adults cannot achieve. With adults the trauma and bad memories can often surface just when a person is beginning to forget. It can often spoil a pleasant experience. Children have shown to recuperate from a terrible experience, such as when a pet dies. Very quickly they can experience new and happy experiences. In Rita's case, the ensuing happy moments with Paul, on balance, took over most of Rita's conscious moments. When bad thoughts arose, she simply replaced them with real and recent experiences.

July 1999

I haven't written in my diary in several months. I found it in my drawer and decided to write something. I find that I don't have anything bad to write about, for a change. For the last few months Paul and I have been seeing each other on a steady basis. I really like Paul and I'm pretty sure he likes me.

COMMENTARY

At this stage of their relationship there was no need to put a label on their relationship. You could say "going steady" or even that they were boyfriend and girlfriend. The contact between their families became more frequent. There are no outstanding circumstances to mar a good thing for both Rita and Paul.

During the summer, in August, Rita and Paul went to the beach with Rita's family and the kids. Rita's brother's wife made sandwiches and Paul bought a cooler filled with ice and sodas. Rita's kids and her brother's kids wee having a great time building sand castles and playing with mud piles. Over time the waves destroyed the sandcastles and they rebuilt them over and over. On this day the beach officials had displayed warnings signs concerning rip currents. Knowing this Paul had said that none of them should not go any further into the water than knee deep. Rita viewed Paul's directions as being "manly" but without even a hint of self praise. Paul's statements usually did not show any signs of problems of obsessiveness about his image. It was a feeling of confidence in who he was. Paul did not seem to require outside appearances of anything he was not. Paul, to his credit knew that there were other men who were better looking, stronger and wiser. It simply didn't matter. In a sub-conscious way he felt content to be somewhat better than average, if not in one way than in another. For a moment Rita did not see J.J. and began to look for him Rita told Paul that she did not know where J.J. was and was beginning to panic. Paul immediately went into the water. It all happened quickly. J.J. was playing in a puddle of water nearby, much to Rita's relief. But just as quickly she lost site of Paul. She called out to Paul but there was no response. She waded into the water, not to deeply, respecting what Paul had said about the rip currents. Rita surprised herself when she felt tears running down her face. Just than Mike called called out to Rita that Paul was about 30 Yards away along the shore. After Telling him that J.J. was safe he told her that he himself had gotten caught by the currents and knew enough not to panic and swim parallel to the current and was able to eventually swim to the shore once away from the rip currents.

Rita and Paul continued seeing each other for the ensuing months. They each became very comfortable with each other. The affection turned from a casual attraction to a sincere love.

In November 1999, they moved in with each other. They rented a nice apartment and were very happy. They enjoyed a great Thanksgiving dinner with both their families and a few days later began to shop for christmas presents.

All in all, their relationship became a loving one. The fear that somehow bad things would begin to happen slowly disappeared. Depending on the degree of suffering and violence, becoming a stable functioning individual can vary as to how much time it takes to achieve.

JANUARY 2000

We had a great Christmas. Thanks to all the help that I received from all the people that helped me. When I re-read the entries on how my life was a living hell, and how It was a torturous life. I'm thankful to the court system that protected me and the counsellors at the shelter especially Joan, I now have the kind of family I always hoped for. I don't know where I would have ended up if not for the help that I got. It all seems now to be in the distant past. The kids have taken to Paul as if he were their Father. I have not heard from Jim again and thats good.

Commentary

A year had gone by and Rita, Paul and the kids were living a normal life, that is to say as normal as any family with good, and not so good times. They had their shares of setbacks with unexpected repairs on Paul's car. and their allotment of colds, fevers and various sore throats.

During 2000, as stated, Rita and Paul were experiencing a very normal life, But what's normal? I choose to define normal as a relationships that are not harmful to anyone. It is the way that most families live, with acceptable problems. Problems that can be worked out amicably without undue hurt feelings.

In June of 2001 the prison guard made noise on the bars of Jim's cell to get his attention. The treatment that he got from the Guards and other prisoners put Jim in a constant feeling of hate towards Rita whom he blamed for his plight. "Come on Jim the lieutenant wants to see you" Jim followed the guard down the metal stairs to the ground floor where there were other cells and a small area for contact with other inmates. "It looks like your going to be released next month" the Lieutenant told Jim. Jim had been a victim of several assaults but otherwise had not been written up as an aggressor. The humiliation he experienced at the hands of other prisoners caused Jim to hate Rita even more. The problem as had been stated previously was that abusers were bullies that generally picked on those that they were was not afraid of. In prison there were many other prisoners that were not afraid of Jim, in fact some thought of Jim as not being as tough as them. Jim wondered if he could meet with Rita when he got out. While hating Rita he had a need to to recover his authority over someone, maybe Rita.

On July 3 2001, Jim was finally released in the custody of a parole officer. Prior to being released, Jim's record had a "flag" indicating that the State attorney's office should be notified of his release. The assistant State Attorney who was assigned to the case called the parole officer to coordinate with him concerning any stipulations as to his release order.

He also contacted the domestic violence prevention office to determine if a restraining order should be filed on behalf of the victim, which in this case was Rita. The order that protected Rita had expired so it was determined that Rita should file for another one just in case.

In some States a restraining order is issued when a person begins his sentence and commences just before his release.

Rita, after being contacted, went to the Domestic Violence intake center where she had originally received her Restraining order. She went reluctantly because she was feeling good about how things had turned out. The advocate proceeded with the same concern as before. The judge signed the restraining order based on the prevued history that was outlined in the petition before. Prior to his release, Jim was served with the new order while still in custody. Deep down inside he was glad that this occurred because he had planned to visit Rita to see if he could continue as before. He had no knowledge about Rita's new life with Paul. He thought that Rita would still be that hopeful girls that he once knew. Jim thought that he would still have power and control over her. Jim was released and was offered residence at a halfway house. Jim was also on probation and was being monitored by the Probation Officer. Aside from being allowed to go to job interviews and to attend a house of worship if he so desired. Also, if he attended any kind of school or sanctioned program.His activity he would be monitored by the probation officer. When he went to a job interviews Jim's appearance and composure was not what the companies wanted from him. Jim didn't care, all he wanted was a chance to go to where Rita lived. Jim stood across the street as long as he thought he could get away with it.He didn't know that Rita no longer lived there. He feared that the probation officer would call the halfway house to check on him. Jim began to formulate a plan to follow Rita home from the courthouse after the Permanent hearing. The hearing was not to happen because the restraining order that the judge signed was for as long as the saw fit to make it. Between drinking bouts and the begging on street corners for money to continue drinking, Jim continued to go to where Rita used to live with her mother. Jim had seen Rita's mother and knew that eventually she would show up. Seeing Rita did not take a long time. On one of the days that Jim loitered around the entrance to Rita's mother's house she showed up to visit. On this day, Jim saw from a distance that Rita was with her mother, her children and someone he did not recognize. A rage began to build up in Jim as he imagined that Rita was not going to need him and looked very happy to be with the man. He saw that the children were sitting close to Paul and that he was very attentive to Rita. Maybe it was at this moment that Jim realized that in spite of all the suffering that he experienced in prison, his life now that he was free, was not going to be any better. Jim, who suffered with undiagnosed depression also probably was undiagnosed with schizophrenia.

That day Rita was with her kids, her mother and Paul and were coming from having lunch at a fast food restaurant. Jim felt that his life was not worth living. His need to have someone to control had continued. His feeling of unworthiness was confusing to him. What seemed clear to Jim was that he did not want Rita to be happy. The rage he now felt was hatred for Rita's new life if not for Rita herself. Outwardly one could surmise that Jim was in a jealous rage but the feeling was complicated. Feelings of need, hatred and despair were intermingled. As is the situation in many cases such as this one, Jim decided that Rita's life should end to pay for what he imagined was her fault.

Jim knew where Rita's mother lived and felt a feeling of accomplishment when he discovered that Rita's mother was still there. Jim figured that eventually Rita would visit. For about a month Jim spent every opportunity to spy on Rita's mother's house. Finally One day Jim saw Rita again arrive at her mother's house along with her children and Paul. The rage that he was increasingly feeling because she was going to be happy with his children and that man. Jim hurriedly went to the halfway house and began to imagine the hurt that Rita would feel as her life ended. He also imagined the hurt that the man and their children would feel. Jim first thought that he would obtain a gun. That at first seemed to be the safest way to do what he was planning. But obtaining a gun was an insurmountable task given that he had no money other than what he acquired by begging at the highway exit. Jim did get to live at the halfway house without having to pay and that included two meals. This arrangement was intended to be a temporary one until he found a job. Jim's thoughts gravitated towards getting a knife. Even if he had the money, he didn't have an idea where to get one. Jim purchased a kitchen knife at a department store. Jim used money that he had begged to buy it. Jim also violated his probation by not returning to the halfway house. On one occasion Jim followed Rita home from her mother's house on a day that she and the children were not with Paul and had to go home by bus. Jim had some change to board the bus, left over from his begging. When he boarded the bus he immediately sat in the front of the bus and never looked back except to glance to see when she would get off. When she did, he did. Rita was concerned with her children and Jim was not in her thoughts. Jim followed her home never allowing her to see him. A few times he had to duck behind a car to avoid having his children see him. Once she got there Jim knew where she would be. all that was left was for Jim to plan what he intended to do.

APRIL, 2000

After giving it some thought, I think that this should be my final entry. The existence of this diary could at this time do more harm than good. It has been my friend throughout my many ordeals and also through my good times that for the most part I'm living today. I'm going to ceremoniously flush it down the toilet page by page. Rita instead just stuck it into the garbage.

Commentary

Jim slept under a bridge with other homeless people. For the most part these were good people that had certain occurrences in their lives that led to their homelessness. Many were abandoned by their family and many had psychological problems, In Jim's case it was that he was a totally dysfunctional person who lived with only one idea and that was to kill Rita. One day in April, Jim decided that the day had come. Jim placed the nine inch knife into his shopping cart where he had all his belongings. No one would recognize Jim with the beard that he had grown. Rita lived with Paul and her children in a apartment complex that was not gated. Had she lived in one with a the security office, the would have had a copy of the restraining order or at least would not have allowed Jim to enter. In this case, Jim simply stayed outside the entry door to the building.

One of the neighbors walked past Jim as she entered the building and asked Jim if he didn't have somewhere else to be. Jim at this point had a scary appearance and answered back in an aggressive manner. Rita's apartment was to the rear of the building and she had no idea that Jim was out there. It's possible that had she seen him, she wouldn't even recognize him. Jim was excited to be in front of Rita's house maybe even delirious. At times he would say a few things to an imaginary person that he thought was with him. all that the imaginary person spoke to Jim about how much he hated Rita and how she was the fault of everything that had happened to him. When the lady that had previously noticed Jim loitering saw him still in front of the building, again talking to himself, she called the police. Jim's demeanor was that of someone building up courage and momentum to do a very terrible act. Not that he had any idea that killing Rita was a bad thing. didn't she deserve it for making him do all the things that got him in trouble. There was the time when he saw Rita show up with Paul and his kids. "She's with a man and with my kids" Jim thought. Jim's mind was reeling. He said to himself "Imagine after all that I did for her, now she's going to have someone else be a father to them." On that occasion he felt the knife at his belt and left muttering to himself. The rest of the day and for the next few days, Jim picked fights with people he met on the street. Finally, on one evening Jim used all the money that he had acquired by begging on a street corner and bought a bottle of cheap whiskey its all he could afford. Jim started drinking and all the while thinking that Rita should have waited for him to get out of prison instead of being with a man. The concept of Rita actually getting married and living a relatively normal life was beyond his understanding. On this day he would get his revenge. On this day he did not see Rita so after being told that if he didn't leave from in front of the building someone told him that they would call the police. Jim went with his shopping cart with his belongings and went to sleep, not in the shelter that the community provided, but under a highway. Jim spent much of the time talking to himself out loud about what he was going was to do to Rita.

Jim awoke from a fretful sleep, waking up about every two hours. Jim grabbed the half empty bottle of whisky, unfortunately the bottle was also half full. After finishing the bottle of whisky he set out for Rita's house. Today was the day, he thought "Today is my day for my revenge." Jim sat against the wall of the building, near the entrance. Jim did not know of Rita's whereabouts or even if she was home. Rita in fact was home with her children who were on their summer vacation. The date was June 5th.

Rita would not see Jim because her windows did not face the front of the building. Others had called the police because he had been seen by some of the people who lived in the building and were becoming suspicious of him. When the police arrived, they spoke to Jim. At this point Jim had convinced the police officers that he was just a homeless man and he did not pose a threat to anyone. They did smell the odor of the whisky that he had been drinking but since he wasn't driving and it was a common enough sight to see semi-drunk men loitering around. The officer ordered Jim to move on, thinking that he would go to a place where they wouldn't be bothered again. Jim started to walk away but the police officer for the record asked Jim for identification. He had none but the officer saw a paper sticking out of his pocket and asked to read it. It was a voucher from the Homeless shelter. The police officer told Jim to go and not to come back. The police officer did not see the knife that Jim had hidden beneath his shirt. Jim thought that he would feign going away but would return as soon as the police left. The police officer ran a check of the name that was on the shelters voucher and two Jim Buchanan's appeared on the computer screen.

One would be a hundred years old but the other fit the description of the Jim that they had speaking to. The screen had the information about Jim's arrest conviction for attempted murder and subsequent prison term. More importantly, for the moment, it had information about the Restraining order that had been issued to him prior to leaving the prison.

The police officer immediately drove the patrol car to the next block where they saw Jim trying not to be seen by standing behind a truck that was parked there. Both officers got out of the police car and approached Jim. The police officer ordered Jim to stand against the wall to check for weapons. What went through Jim's crazed mind was that he was not going to go back to jail, not without getting even with Rita. He thought that he would rather be killed by the police officer if he was going to go to jail and Rita was going to be happy with someone else. Jim suddenly took his knife from his belt and lunged at the police officer. he also had this warped notion that maybe he could somehow get away. The police officer stepped back and drew his weapon from its holster and fired one shot striking Jim on his chest. The paramedics were called but Jim had expired before their arrival.

Rita never heard the commotion since it occurred a block away. She went about her business being a mother and someone who was in a functioning relationship. There was a small article in the newspaper that day but Rita did no read or even see it. Someone did mention the incident in passing but it simply did not register with Rita that it had to do with a domestic violence incident.

Final Commentary

There was a television police show in the fifties where the narrater Would say at the end of the show "There are eight million cases in the naked city, this was one of them" or something to that effect.

This too could have ended in an untold number of ways. In the approximately fifteen thousand cases that I assisted in securing safety for persons who were experiencing abusive behavior, violence and danger to her and possibly to her loved ones. Most cases did not end as tragically as the one described. Fortunately when it appeared that the victim needed to get away, escape if you will, there needed to be a place and a method where the victim could go to seek help.

Combatting Abuse by one individual against another has a history that one does not have to go to far back to discover.

In ancient time in some cultures it was perfectly normal to abuse and harm ones partner, married or not. Even worse, in some cultures it was actually legal to do so. We as a culture should not imagine that we are above having a problem of spousal or relational abuse. Up into recently, the physical violence was viewed by law enforcement to be a "family matter" Fortunately civility triumphed and that is no longer the case. In the end a societies level of civility can be measured by how it helps those that are incapable of helping themselves.

Not always can a victim up and leave, in fact when a person decides to leave it could be possibly the most dangerous time. There actually are many complications in seeking their safety. The victim may not have the means to do so. In many cases the abuser does not allow the victim to drive a car. Sometimes he does not allow the victim have friends that can help them. Also in some cases they are not allowed to have a relationship with their family. One very important point to know is that those that are willing to help a person being abused is that the victim has to leave the abuser when its safe to do so. Studies have shown that the most dangerous time to leave a violent abusive relationship is when the victim decides, indeed, to escape. At the thought that the abuser is going to lose his power, he more than likely will go into a rage. These rages coupled with alcohol and drug abuse exacerbates the situation and even worse if a mental condition is present it can cause the situation to become tragic. If you know someone who is being physically abused you should gain her trust by being a compassionate listener. Let her know that she should seek the help of a trained advocate that can assist her through the various entities that exist. Later, I will include an emergency telephone number to call for help. In every community in America there are organizations that can help acquire the needed assistance, become familiar with these telephone numbers. The assistance is more than just getting away, more often than not there also needs to be a way to not need to return to the abusive and dangerous situation. Beside the initial court order to make it unlawful for the abuser to have any contact with the victim, thus giving her a chance to arranged for her safety. there are other matters such as emergency shelter, food and clothing for the children. Often, the victim can be awarded exclusive use of the home they shared when the judge deems it to be appropriate. Friends and family or someone who has noticed that this violence is occurring and feels a need, because of caring, to help the victim and her children stay safe should assist her. Its always good to have an emergency plan and especially have a method of communicating, with caring person alarming situation.

It's advised that the victim keep, if possible an amount of money to pay for emergency food and shelter for her and her children. At least until she obtains the assistance that is available, that has been discussed. Also to keep safe important documents. The police can assist by informing the victim of where to call to obtain help. Generally the police can give the victim literature with information that she can use. Also if there is criminal activity being perpetrated, they can initiate law enforcement procedures.

Throughout this discourse, I have used women as the victim. This was done as a manner of convenience.

The fact is that domestic violence can and does occur against men. domestic violence effect persons from all walks of society. Gay, lesbian, wealthy and poor. Also against the elderly and those that are most vulnerable.

As a society we have come a long way. From a time when there was absolutely no help at all to a time when there were many avenues of assistance to combat domestic violence including the Police, State Attorney's, Judges, Shelters, Advocates and the many socially minded organizations both private and faith inspired.

It's important to note that what occurred to the fictional Rita was my opinion based on my advocating for about fifteen thousand victims of domestic abuse and involving persons related and/non-related including against children, the elderly and other situations that are not considered familial. The main intention was an attempt to answer the question as to why do people in abusive relationships stay in it. By reading Rita's entries into her diary, the reader could get an idea of what she was thinking.

It should be also noted that nothing written here is intended to serve as legal advise. Questions of a legal nature should be addressed to an attorney. Certainly contact with a local advocacy group would be a good first step. And finally, in all situations involving an immediate danger the Police should be contacted.

Most of what has been written concerning procedures was true at the time of this writing. keeping in mind that many factors related here can and does vary from state to state.

The National Domestic Violence Hotline is as of this writing: 1-800-799-7233 and 1-800-787-3224 for the hearing impaired (TTY)

One last thought. Truly loving ones partner is a major factor in every relationship, and if there are problems that cause to people to part, I'm reminded of a little poem I wrote many years ago.

Like a wounded, beautiful little blue bird, I have nurtured lovingly.

And then when your able to fly, I'll open my palm and let you fly away. If you come back, you bring with you the sunshine and blue skies-the sweet smell of springtime, the bliss and joy of the happiness I once knew.

If you don't I will pray that you find the branches - up high - where the air is clean and your nest can be shared with those that can bring you the happiness that you deserve. And that the top of the trees offer you an abundance of all the good things that life up there can offer you.

Through the grey skies and shadows that are cast upon me, I will always remember the softness of your feathers upon my face- the gentleness by which I held you and the tenderness of the quivering in my hand, and the knowledge that you will, from time to time, remember the warmth of my hand.